# sneakers

Samuel
Americus
Walker

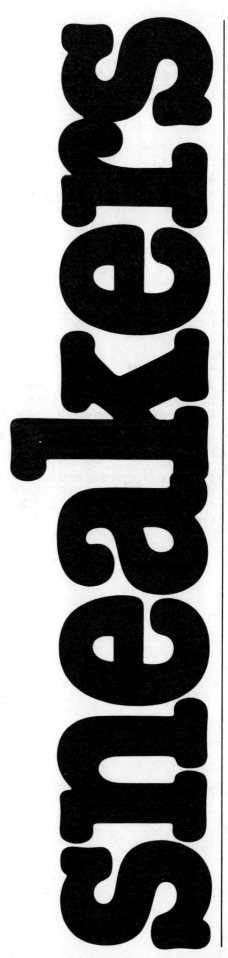

sneakers

Workman
Publishing
New York

Cover and book design: Paul Hanson

Workman Publishing Company
1 West 39 Street
New York, New York 10018

Manufactured in the United States of America
First printing June 1978
10  9  8  7  6  5  4  3  2  1

Library of Congress Cataloging in Publication Data

Walker, Samuel Americus.
    Sneakers.

    1. Sneakers—Addresses, essays, lectures.
I. Title.
GV749.S64W54       685.3       77-18425
ISBN 0-89480-016-7

## Acknowledgments

Roberta Bayley; Edo Bertoglio; Bleecker Bob; Robert and Rhett
Brown; Neke Carson; Carlsen Import Shoe Co.; Scott Cohen; Donna
Dennis; Josh Ellis, *Solters & Roskin*; Charles Flanagan, *New Balance*;
John Haskell, *Professional Marketing Group*; Jack Hawkins, *Uniroyal*;
Mark Jacobsen; Ray Johnson; Jill Kornblee; Jessie LaSar, *Athlete's
Foot*; Ellen Leventhal; Marty Liquori; Bill Lyon, *Converse*; Don
McGee, *PF*; James McPadden; Peter Meltzer; John L. Powers; Josh
Rabinowitz, *CITC*; William A. Rossi; Mr. Sharhiman, *Malaysian
Rubber Bureau*; Gail Sicilia; Kate Simon; Stanley Sterenberg, *Athlete's
Foot*; Bart Stolp, *Adidas*; Lynn Strong; Ruth Tannenhaus, *Museum of
Contemporary Crafts*; Michelle Urry; Rodger J. Winn, M.D.

To B. B. W.
Neither old hat, nor old shoe.

# The shoe that conquered the world

**A** whole book devoted to sneakers? "Who would be interested?" said our wing-tipped, stiletto-heeled, cowboy-booted, penny-loafered friends.

"Follow us," we said, and took them for a morning jog, an afternoon of tennis and an early evening squash match.

"Keep looking," we said, as we marched them 'round the jungle gym, though the schoolyard, across the Quad and off to the rock concert.

"Focus on the feet," we said, and handed them enough popcorn to sit through a triple-feature of *Oh, God, Rocky,* and a rerun of *West Side Story.*

"Admire the artwork," we said, carting them off to the museum where Oldenburg's Giant Gym Shoes and Lichtenstein's pop art sneaks hung, and Andy Warhol walked by wearing paint-splattered sneakers of his own.

"Eyes down," we said, as Woody Allen raced past.

"Now, up," we said, as a gorgeous Monaco princess whizzed by in a T-shirt with a sneaker appliqué.

"Not through yet," we said, as we sat them behind the shoe store cash register, where 50 percent of the sales tallied were for a new pair of sneaks.

"Ready to call it a night?" we finally said, then tucked them into a sneaker-shaped bed and rested our case.

The answer to who is interested in sneakers is obviously "everybody." If you own feet, you not only need them, you lust for them—it's just that simple. In fact, in the United States over 200 million pairs of sneakers are sold every year. Sneaks have become indispensable. They are as much our way of life as T-shirts, Cokes and big, friendly smiles, all of which turn up at almost every occasion.

Long gone are the days sneaks came in just two colors—black or white—and just two styles—high-cut or low. Dimly remembered are the times when sneaks were only fit for gym workouts and garage cleanouts. And almost as hard to recall are the years when sneaks stayed on the feet. (Now they appear as necklace pendants, wall hangings, tote bags, even bookends.)

Who can explain a phenomenon? We'd be foolish to try. The only thing we can remind you of is this: Have you ever known anybody who *didn't* own a pair of sneakers?

Some of us are very sentimental about our favorite form of footwear. We love buying new ones, but we hate to part with old ones. We think of them as friends.

Here, now, the story of sneakers, from the Victorian croquet sandal to the modern racing flat.

We guarantee it won't chafe, blister, pinch or rub you the wrong way.

# Contents

# Sneaker anatomy

# Sneaker game plan

# Sneaker fashion

# Sneaker art

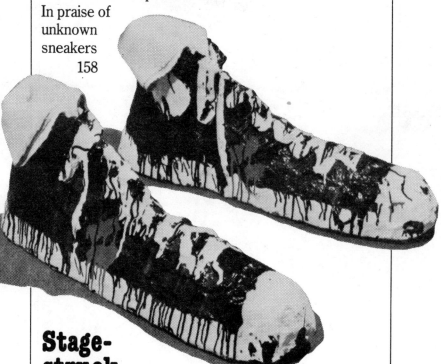

# Stage-
# struck
# sneakers

# Sneaker care

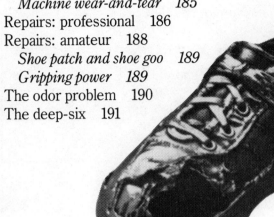

# sneaker history

# The first sneaker

**I**t prefers to remain anonymous.

Nobody's sure who made it, who purchased it or what it actually looked like.

But we do know that on May 19, 1832, Wait Webster of New York was granted a U.S. patent for his process of "attaching India Rubber soles to boots and shoes," and he must have been thinking sneaker-type thoughts when he applied for it.

And we've also learned that the Candee Company of New Haven, Connecticut, was the first manufacturer licensed to make footwear using the Goodyear vulcanization process (without which there'd be no such thing as a sneaker).

So it's reasonable to assume that the little gleam in their collective eye wasn't much different from the item that was finally produced in 1868. This had a rubber sole, a canvas upper, laces — all the things we recognize as standard sneak equipment.

Only trouble is, it was called a "croquet sandal."

The idle rich adored it. When they tired of croquet, they took it to their beach pavilions or to the club for a quiet set of tennis. No need to ask if this upper-crust delight was expensive. Of course it was. The Peck and Snyder Sporting Goods Catalog listed it in the $6 range.

By 1873 it no longer traveled incognito. Ads revealed its true name — sneaker. At which point the masses decided they weren't intimidated by it, and in 1897 even Sears, Roebuck offered the item for a mere $.60. Sneakers became *the* gym shoe. Things aren't really so different these days, are they?

*Baby foot (size 2) and big foot (size 22).*

# Victorian excesses

**A**lthough they could be lured to the tennis court, turn-of-the-century ladies were hardly expected to give up their silk and satin trimmings. Peeking out from beneath many an ankle-length skirt was a fragile bow, anchored to the sneaker by its owner's persistent refusal to move—no matter where the ball landed.

Their gentlemen friends were no less stylish in black sateen sneakers with elkskin trim (highly polished for the day's outing by the downstairs servants). White "duck" canvas high-tops were another period favorite often seen on the approach to a sticky wicket.

*During the Victorian era there were no less than nineteen sneaker manufacturers. Eventually, all but 3 joined to form U.S. Royal. Some of these early relics are probably still residing in attic trunks. If the dust has not obliterated their trademarks by now, you may be able to see the names of Goodyear Glove, National India Rubber Company, Champion, Lycoming, Keystone, B.F. Goodrich or Spalding on them. In which case, you've probably got yourself a genuine sneaker heirloom.*

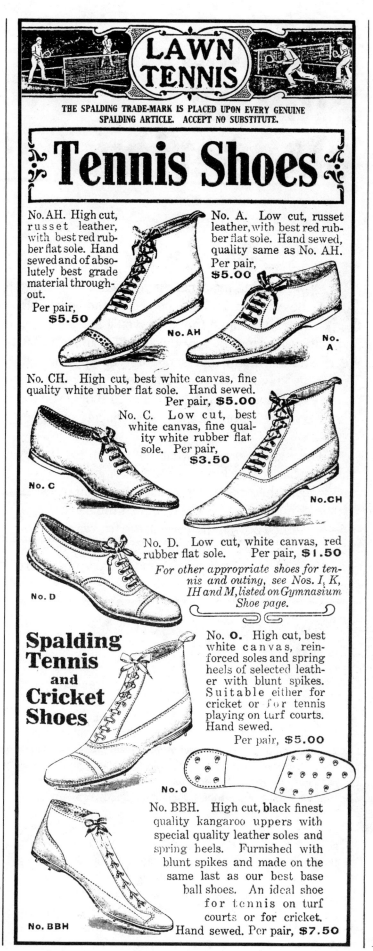

# LAWN TENNIS

# Tennis Shoes

**No. AH.** High cut, russet leather, with best red rubber flat sole. Hand sewed and of absolutely best grade material throughout.
Per pair, **$5.50**

**No. A.** Low cut, russet leather, with best red rubber flat sole. Hand sewed, quality same as No. AH.
Per pair, **$5.00**

**No. CH.** High cut, best white canvas, fine quality white rubber flat sole. Hand sewed.
Per pair, **$5.00**

**No. C.** Low cut, best white canvas, fine quality white rubber flat sole. Per pair, **$3.50**

**No. D.** Low cut, white canvas, red rubber flat sole. Per pair, **$1.50**

*For other appropriate shoes for tennis and outing, see Nos. I, K, IH and M, listed on Gymnasium Shoe page.*

## Spalding Tennis and Cricket Shoes

**No. O.** High cut, best white canvas, reinforced soles and spring heels of selected leather with blunt spikes. Suitable either for cricket or for tennis playing on turf courts. Hand sewed.
Per pair, **$5.00**

**No. BBH.** High cut, black finest quality kangaroo uppers with special quality leather soles and spring heels. Furnished with blunt spikes and made on the same last as our best base ball shoes. An ideal shoe for tennis on turf courts or for cricket. Hand sewed. Per pair, **$7.50**

# Life on a rubber plantation

**P**retend you've gotten your hands on H.G. Wells' time machine. Sit yourself down, facing the Amazon, and set the dial for the year 1736. When you open the door, you'll find a French expedition hacking its way through the jungle in 90° heat. You join them, but suddenly you spy Indians. With large knives. And very funny feet. The members of the expedition are impressed, and so should you be, because you're staring at the first producers of rubber shoes.

The Indians explain what they're up to. If they slash the bark of the hevea tree, out comes the sap—a milky liquid they call caoutchouc, which you translate as "tears of the wood." They deposit the sap in large, open-mouthed bowls, then attack the tricky part of the process. To shape the substance into shoes, they dip their feet into the bowls and stand in front of the fire

## The man who stole the rubber seeds

**T**he first merchants to move into the Amazon and establish rubber plantations were more interested in making overnight fortunes than in caring for their valuable trees. As a result, the supply of rubber soon dwindled and prices skyrocketed. Finally, one English planter, Henry Wickham, exposed the situation in a book called *A Journey Through the Wilderness*. The British Empire's India office took notice and helped Wickham circumvent the Brazilian export laws by bringing out a large quantity of seeds disguised as orchids. The seeds were sown in London's Kew Gardens greenhouses, and from there rubber plants were shipped to tropical locales throughout the Empire, particularly in India and Southeast Asia. By the early twentieth century, Asia had become the source of most of the world's rubber—at a price sneaker-wearers could afford.

until it hardens. Which explains why their feet looked so odd at first sight; they were encased in great lumps of rubber. These "gumboats" have several advantages: they're waterproof, they fit perfectly and they can be "resoled" by redipping.

It soon becomes clear that the Brazilian Indians have a monopoly on this style of footwear. They're the only ones who own rubber trees and their rubber is not transportable — after a few days, it congeals into a

*A worker extracting latex with a special knife called a "rubber tapper."*

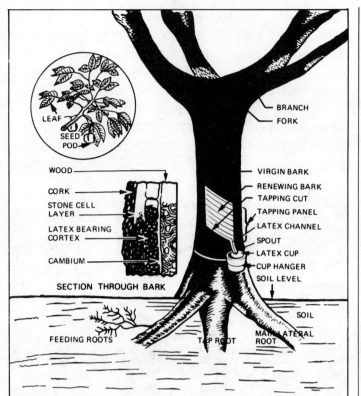

Courtesy The Malaysian Rubber Producers' Research Association

*A mature rubber tree is anywhere from 30 to 60 feet tall and is productive for approximately twenty-five years.*

useless blob. The French are dismayed, but word gets to England, where they find a use for it in a different form. Joseph Priestley discovers that the material is excellent for rubbing off pencil marks. He formally dubbs it "rubber" and the eraser industry is born.

Time speeds ahead to 1819. Rubber shoes still seem an impossibility, but London manufacturer Thomas Hancock invents the "pickle"—a machine that chews on rubber until it's soft enough to be turned into rubber thread. The underwear trade is ecstatic. Five years later, Charles Mackintosh, a Scot, figures out how to liquefy rubber with naphtha and thereby invents the modern raincoat—called "Mac" in his honor.

Meanwhile, back on the plantation, the natives try to hang on to their rubber trees, which for reasons they don't understand seem to be in great demand all over the globe. They pass a law making it illegal to take the trees out of the country. Even so, seeds find their way to India and Malaysia, and Brazil is no longer the world's chief rubber supplier.

As it turns out, the Indians needn't have been so greedy. After Charles Goodyear stumbled on the vulcanization process (which made rubber suitable for shoe manufacture), the demand for rubber was so huge, that they would have been hard put to keep up

with it.

# Sneaker chronology

**1868** First rubber-soled canvas shoe manufactured

**1873** Term "sneaker" coined

**1892** U.S. Rubber Company incorporated

**1897** Sears' catalog offers black sateen sneaks, 60¢; white canvas sneaks, $1

**1908** Marquis M. Converse opens workroom

**1909** Leather basketball shoes introduced

**1910** Spalding adds suction cups to soles

**1915** U.S. Navy Department orders first G.I. sneaks

**1917** Keds and Converse All-Stars introduced

**1920** Duke of Windsor brings white tennis shoes into fashion; wears them on visit to U.S.

**1925** Dassler Sports Shoes founded (forerunner of Adidas and Puma)

**1929** Spalding introduces arch cushion; Keds, colored soles

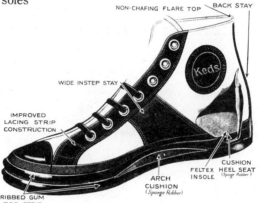

**1934** Keds introduces colored uppers

**1935** Blue canvas sneaks accepted on tennis courts

**1942** Synthetic rubber developed

**1948** Adi Dassler forms Adidas; Rudolph Dassler, Puma

Courtesy Adidas

**1950** Side ventilating eyelets introduced

**1965** Composition soles popularized

**1968** Sneaker boom commences

**1972** Waffle sole revolutionizes running shoes

# The father of the sneaker

**I**n 1834 Charles Goodyear, a hardware seller, noticed a rubber life preserver in a store window. Upon investigating, he learned that the rubber melted in hot weather and cracked in the cold. This presented a challenge, and Goodyear borrowed money to finance some experiments. Despite the fact that his research led to several stints in debtors' prison and a life of poverty for his family, he persevered in the belief that rubber could be stabilized.

*Charles Goodyear, 1800–1860.*

Eventually, Goodyear hired Nathaniel Hayward to assist him. Hayward had found that rubber mixed with sulfur and exposed to sunlight would harden—but only on the surface. Goodyear purchased the rights to this process, but it was not until 1839—when he accidentally dropped a rubber-and-sulfur mixture containing white lead onto the hot stove—that he discovered the secret of vulcanization. In 1844 he was granted a patent for the now-perfected process and again found himself in a financial quandary—this time because of legal entanglements. Finally, in 1852, the patent was confirmed, and Goodyear set out to establish a rubber industry in Europe. He failed in England, and three years later, after his French company went bankrupt, he was once again imprisoned for debts.

Alas, Charles Goodyear never lived to see his godchild—the sneaker.

*A modern vulcanizer. After an hour and a half in it, your sneakers are ready.*

# Sneaker scrapbook

**1922.** Class B champions. Winner wears black low-cuts, runner-up prefers white and fawn high-tops.

Culver Pictures, Inc.

**1918.** *The U.S. Navy basketball team wears 14 ounce two-tone sneaks, with reinforced toe box.*

Culver Pictures, Inc

**1920.** *Keds features the "Sister Sue" pump for young ladies.*

**1931.** *Lillywhites, a London department store, offers this canvas beach shoe for 12'6.*

**1935.** *Navy blue becomes the color for boating sneaks. Land-lubbers adopt blue as well, but also travel about in brown, red, light blue, maroon and gray sneaks. "Tire duck" canvas is popularized for uppers. Its devotees extol its coolness. Winter sneaks, however, forego canvas for the warmth of corduroy.*

**1940.**
*The "Radcliffe"
goes o,f to
college.*

Keds
REG. U.S. PAT. OFF.
SHOCK·PROOF
Insole

**1934.**
Keds introduces
the shock-proof
insole, patents it
and designs a logo
to promote it.

**1930.** *Converse features a
Boston Bulldog in its
advertising campaign for
Skoots, "Canvas shoes
for every sport."*

**1932.** *The Converse Basketball Yearbook debuts. It features articles and
photographs on game technique and strategy, famous players who swear by
their All-Stars. Early Yearbooks are hard to come by. Best chance of finding
them is to inherit them. The Yearbook is still published today, with an emphasis on Converse basketball clinics and the super stars who participate in
them.*

**1917.** *The all-mighty All-Star
makes its first basket.*

# BIKE KEDS

**1934.** *Keds presents pigskin-trimmed biking sneaks, suggests they be worn for roller skating and classroom activity, too.*

**1922.** *Keds announces "Field Days," competitions open to anyone wearing their sneaks. Fun! Prizes! Fame! Handbills distributed to all interested parties.*

SAY KIDS!

A $50 "ROLLFAST"
**BICYCLE** **FREE!**
WILL BE GIVEN AWAY
Every Boy Buying A Pair Of
**KEDS**
**BIKE ABSOLUTEL**
ALSO
9 OTHER VALUABLE
BICYCLE ON DISPLAY AT O
**BOSTON SHOE**
547-49 Landis Avenue

Keds Week
May 20th to May 27th

WIN
a WIRE HAIRED
FOX TERRIER

There's a free copy of the new Keds Handbook for every boy and girl who come in to this store during Keds Week. Learn how you can enter the Keds Wire Haired Terrier Contest, too. Nothing to buy or sell.

Join the Pirate Ship Contest
AT YOUR UNDERSELLING STORE
OUR OWN C
Starts Tuesd
Three Prizes Absol
FIRST PRIZE—Larg
SECOND PRIZE—On
THIRD PRIZE—On
NOTHING
Come in and get a co
blank. You might
Warsa

Keds Week
May 20th to 27th

WIN
A WIRE HAIRED
FOX TERRIER or
A NEW BICYCLE

There's a free copy of the Keds Handbook for every boy and girl who comes to the Junior Basement Shoe Section during this week. Learn how you can enter the Keds contest, too nothing to buy or sell.
—Basement Shoes.

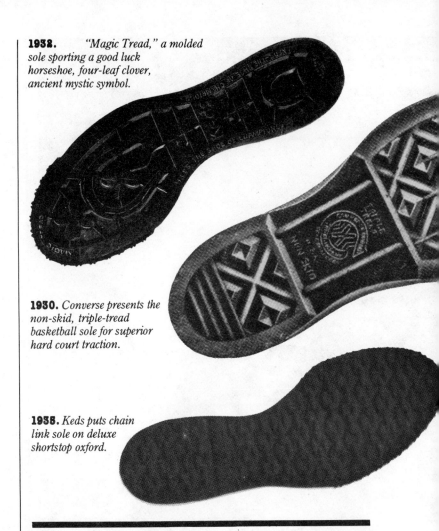

**1932.** *"Magic Tread," a molded sole sporting a good luck horseshoe, four-leaf clover, ancient mystic symbol.*

**1930.** *Converse presents the non-skid, triple-tread basketball sole for superior hard court traction.*

**1935.** *Keds puts chain link sole on deluxe shortstop oxford.*

**1930.** *P.F. "Flyers" thrived. Color was added to rubber compounds for the first time, making "marbelized" sole combinations possible. Principal selling point was the sneaker sole's traction pattern, giving rise to such designs as diamonds, weaves, links, woven basket motifs, feathers, even swirls.*

28 | **1937.** *From the Keds catalogue.*

Non-Heat
Insole

$1.19
Juvenile

**"Mickey Mouse" White Canvas Shoes**
Mickey Mouse imprint. Black trimmed lace stay; back stay, saddle straps. Ankle patch; reinforced toe guard. Crepe rubber outsole, rubber foxing. Sizes and half sizes. State size.
**6 F 1309**—Boys' sizes, 2½ to 8. $1.25
Shpg. wt., 2 lbs. 2 oz.
**6 F 1311**—Juvenile sizes, 11 to 2.
Shpg. wt., 1 lb. 12 oz. ..............$1.19

**1934.** *Sears' catalogue accepted mail-orders for the Mickey Mouse high-top.*

**1932.** *Montgomery Ward's catalogue offered a variety of basketball sneaks, none more popular than "Dutch's."*

## The Shoe of Champions
### *Nationally Famous*
## "DUTCH" LONBORG
## Basketball Shoe

Northwestern University's Team Wears Them!

**● FEATURES ●**
—Designed by "Dutch" Lonborg, basketball coach of Northwestern University.
—Sponge rubber cushion heel.
—Keneva non-heat insole.
—Gray rubber non-slip sole.
—Stubber toe guards.
—Heavy khaki Army duck uppers.

Uppers of heavyweight flexible khaki colored army duck with one-piece, non-wrinkling loose lining. Extra thick brown rubber scuffer toe cap. One-piece tongue, gray inside lining. Heavy brown rubber stubber toe guards. Built-in **arch support.** Heavy gray compounded rubber soles —easy to start—sprint—stop—or pivot quickly—on any floor. State size. Order half size smaller than street shoe. **Postpaid.**
**60 E 4982**—For Men SIZES: 6½ to 12. Per pair .......... $2.98
TEAM LOT—Five or more pairs. Per pair, **2.89**
**60 E 4983**—For Boys—SIZES: 2½ to 6. Per pair .......... **2.75**
TEAM LOT—Five or more pairs. Per pair **2.65**

$2.98
Pair
Postpaid

Double
Toe
Cap

Gray
Non-Slip
Sole

Army Duck Uppers

New
Non-Heat
Insole

Sponge
Rubber
Cushion
Heel

**"BIG TEN" Championship Cup**
Northwestern University's Basketball team, wearing the "Dutch" Lonborg Shoe in all games, won this cup in 1931—runner-up in 1932. Our manufacturers retain "Dutch" Lonborg, coach of this famous team, in designing this shoe. His autograph on each pair is his seal of approval.

**1959.** *Twenty-five men board a tiny motor scooter and go for a ride in Burgos, Spain. At 500 feet all fell off.*

United Press International

**1975.** *A celebrity auction was held at the Manhattan Theater Club. Famous personalities were asked to donate an object of either real or sentimental value, and talk show host Dick Cavett chose to part with his sneaks. From all reports, they were well-worn. No one knows what's become of them, including Mr. Cavett.*

Ken Howard

*1974. "Wall-walking" becomes the craze at colleges.*

**Late 1940's.** *People in the Boston area tuned in WGBH just to hear what zany Bob and Ray would come up with next. Once, they offered oyster-filled sneakers as the prize. Listeners liked the idea so much that Bob and Ray repeated the gimmick many times. "If you win," they told the audience, "don't tell us your size. We prefer to guess."*

*1972. Udderly beguiling.*

# Sneaker snobbery

**B**e it ever so humble, it's still not a sneaker. Not these days. Sure, it may look like one to you—with its comfy upper and its trusty sole—but that's not what the stuck-ups call it. To them, it's a jogging shoe, a training shoe, a pair of flats. A tennis shoe, a squash shoe, perhaps a leisure shoe. A basketball shoe, a volleyball shoe, or at the very least, an all-purpose athletic shoe. But a lowly sneaker? Never!

Admittedly, the ones you'd run in to win the Boston Marathon aren't quite the thing for an overhead smash at Wimbledon. But that doesn't mean they're any less a sneaker.

What's the matter with the word, anyway? It's got a good old Anglo-Saxon root—*snaca,* from the Latin noun for "snake." *Snican* described the way the *snaca* moved, and it slithered into English as the verb "to sneak" almost four centuries ago. It became our favorite shoe, the sneaker, in 1873 when it was offered for sale in a mail-order catalog.

Just remember. You're wearing sneakers. And anyone who tries to tell you otherwise is misguided.

## Sneaker synonyms

Felony shoes     Tennies
Gumshoes     Tractor treads
Gym shoes
Perpetrator boots
Plimsolls
Pussyfooters
Sneaks

*A 1937 Keds.*

Courtesy Uniroyal

# The royal sneaker

**B**limey, it's the Duke in plimsolls. Aboard his yacht. Sipping tea on the garden lawn. Even visiting the Colonies. "Plimsoll" refers back to the Englishman, Samuel Plimsoll, who proposed the Merchant Shipping Act of 1876, one of whose provisions was that ships must be marked with safe waterlines to avoid overloading. These lines, to English eyes, resembled those on sneaker soles—and sneakers became plimsolls.

*The Prince of Wales playing tennis in Venice.*

# The political sneaker

## Democrat

34 | *Carter playing with the Secret Service.*

# Republican

*Ford taking a break at Camp David.*

# Working class sneakers

One of the senior editors at a large New York publishing house always wears sneakers to the office. Scuttlebutt has it, that's his way of thumbing his nose at convention.

In the city room of the Boston *Globe,* if a reporter says, "Sneakers wants to see you," you better march yourself over to the managing editor and ask him what he wants. The staff calls him that—behind his back—because he wears sneaks every single day.

Obviously, both these men suffer no qualms about putting sneaks in a business situation. But then, they're awfully good at their jobs and it would be pretty hard to fire them. Unless you're indispensable, too, and an executive, you better not try getting away with it. Remember what happened to Ted Baxter.

Baxter, the tactless newscaster on *The Mary Tyler Moore Show,* appeared at a conference in the station manager's office in a natty three-piece suit. And white canvas sneakers. He thought the combination would impress his boss — show him he was businesslike, yet casual. Throughout the meeting, the chief's eyes were riveted on Ted's shoes. "Ted," he finally said, "I have just one question for you. *Why are you wearing sneakers, Ted? Tell me that, why?"* Baxter, now aware that he'd made a terrible faux pas, harrumphed and hawed and then managed to squeak out, "I have a lot of running around to do."

One last footnote: If you're determined to wear sneaks on the job, take on City Hall. At the tender age of seventy-four, Isabella W. Cannon decided to run for mayor of Raleigh, North Carolina. Her campaign image was "the little old lady in tennis shoes." From one end of town to the other, she solicited votes in them—in schoolyards, parking lots, shopping centers, even factory sites. She won the election. And she now wears sneaks to the office.

*Sneaks to go. At Butterfly Bob's Salad Bar in Seattle, luncheon deliveries are whisked to nearby offices by co-owner Bob Snyder, dressed as you see him here. Your sandwich is stashed in his wings. Most messengers dress a bit more conservatively, but they, too, wear sneakers —the ultimate shoe to go.*

United Press International

38 | *The New York Police, working out in "Felony Shoes."*

# sneaker manufacture

# Visit to a sneaker factory

Crude rubber awaiting the guillotine, a machine which works like a kitchen chopper but with sixty-five tons of pressure.

The press room, where insoles and heel and arch cushions are cut from foam rubber sheets.

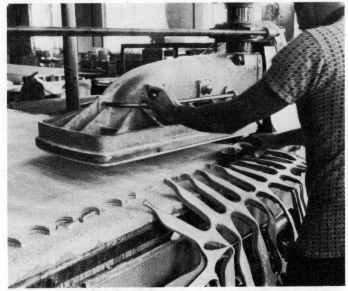

Uppers being dye-cut from layers of canvas.

Gluing cushions to insoles as they move along a conveyor belt.

Foam padding being inserted in the collar of a leather upper.

The glue bath.

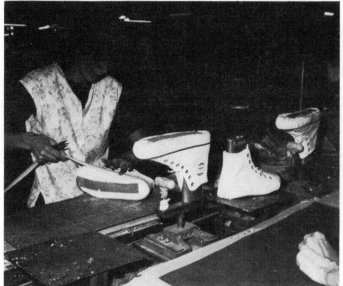

A foxing strip is wrapped around the sneak.

Upside-down sneaks, showing arch cushions newly attached to insoles.

Pressing the outsole in place.

Roughing up the insole and upper bottom so the glue will adhere better.

44  Activating the glue by heating the uppers.

Sneaks, still on their metal lasts, ready to roll into the vulcanizer. (Leather sneaks don't get to make the trip, nor do most running shoes. They don't require vulcanization.)

The vulcanizer interior, where soles are bonded to uppers in about an hour-and-a-half.

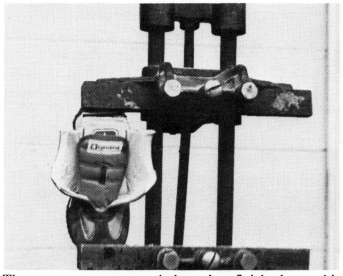

The torture test, to judge the finished sneak's flexibility.

# The basic sneak

## Uppers:

**Lace to toe** The quickest way to tell if your sneak follows this format is to count the eyelets. Less than four to a side and it probably doesn't. The laces butt the toe box, then continue smack to the ankle. Hi-tops feature a lace-to-toe design, as do most basketball shoes.

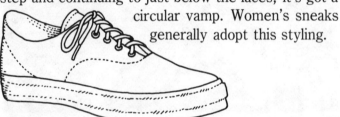

**Circular vamp** If your sneak looks as if it's joined by stitching in a nice, rounded curve beginning at the instep and continuing to just below the laces, it's got a circular vamp. Women's sneaks generally adopt this styling.

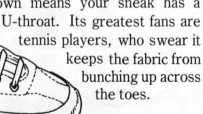

**U-throat** Lacing that seems to sit in a squared-off box on their own means your sneak has a U-throat. Its greatest fans are tennis players, who swear it keeps the fabric from bunching up across the toes.

**Saddle** Found only on New Balance athletic shoes, the saddle features two separate strips which support either side of the instep. In theory, this gives better fit, lessening the sneak's tendency to gap.

46

Fred Winkowski

# Soles:

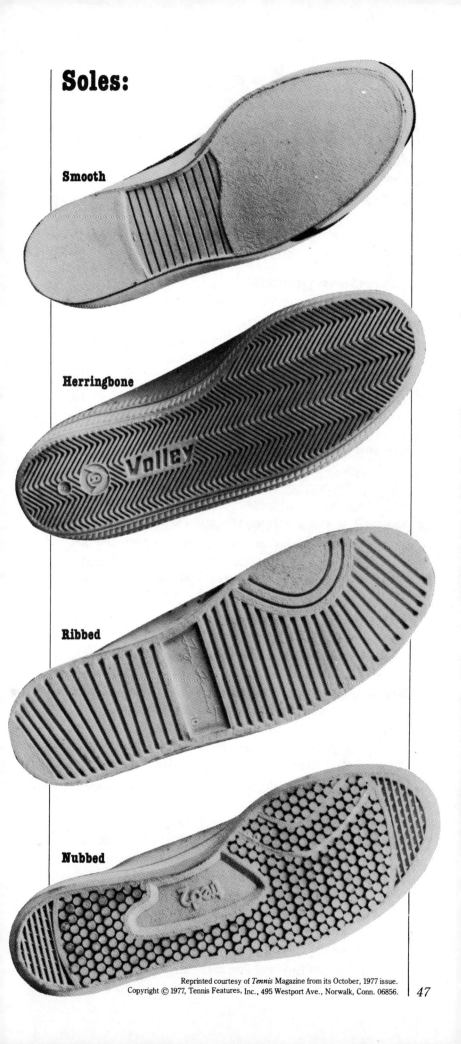

**Smooth**

**Herringbone**

**Ribbed**

**Nubbed**

# Sneaker glossary

**Achilles tendon protector:** A raised cushion at the back of the heel, common to most low-cut running, tennis and basketball shoes.

**Arch cushion:** A support for the arch of the foot. Some experts object that its positioning is incorrect for this purpose.

**Bumper:** An extra strip of rubber attached to the toe for cushioning impact, particularly on basketball, tennis or hard-court shoes.

**Binding:** The reinforced part of the upper, usually at the edge of the canvas or leather. The upper fabric may be simply turned over and stitched, or padding may be added.

**Collar:** The open part of the shoe where the foot is inserted. Today, many sneakers, especially basketball and tennis shoes, feature padded collars.

**Elevated heel:** Found on better athletic shoes. Saves strain on the Achilles tendon, the ankle and the heel of the foot.

**Eyelets:** The small holes through which the laces are inserted. Most eyelets are reinforced with metal or plastic.

**Flared heel:** A widened heel to distribute the stress of impact when the heel of the foot hits the ground.

**Foxing:** A thin rubber tape bonding the upper to the sole. Provides support for the side of the foot.

**Heel counter:** Grips the heel of the foot to keep it from moving inside the sneaker. Usually made of plastic or leather.

**Hi-cut:** A sneaker that rises over the ankle.

**Injection molding:** The process of setting the upper into a mold of the outsole, then injecting liquid soling material (usually PVC) into the mold to bond the sole to the upper. Used primarily in low-cost sneakers.

**Insole:** The cushioned pad, most often foam rubber, on which the foot rests. Sometimes features extra padding at the heel and arch, and may be covered with canvas, nylon or terry cloth.

# Sneaker cross section

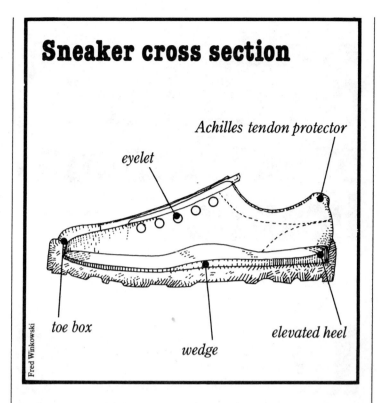

Achilles tendon protector

eyelet

toe box

wedge

elevated heel

Fred Winkowski

**Last:** The foot form around which a shoe is built. Lasts are metal for vulcanized shoes, plastic for most other types.

**Low-cut:** A sneaker that does not rise over the ankle.

**Midsole:** Extra padding between the insole and the outsole. A feature of modern running shoes.

**Outsole:** The part of the sole that comes in contact with the ground. Most running shoes feature a tough surface layer added on to the standard rubber or plastic outsole.

**Slip-sole:** The process of gluing and stitching premade soles to the uppers. Used to make most good athletic shoes that are not vulcanized.

**Suction cups:** Added to outsoles for traction on smooth surfaces such as basketball courts.

**Toe box:** The part of the sneaker that encases the toes.

**Toe cap:** Additional protection on the toe of the shoe. Rubber is used for basketball and tennis shoes, suede or leather for running shoes.

**Tongue:** A flap that starts at the toe and covers the instep under the lacing area. Today, many sneakers have tongues through which the lace can pass once so they can be held in place.

**Upper:** The top of the shoe.

**Vamp:** The part of the upper encompassing the lacing area. Provides most of the support to the instep.

**Wedge:** A layer of cushioned rubber that provides extra padding under the arch and heel. A feature of most running shoes.

# Keds, Connies and other famous brands

**I**magine walking into a shoe store, cornering the clerk and demanding to see "a National India Rubber Company sneaker, please." Quite a mouthful, isn't it? The Company thought so, too, and in 1917 decided on something snappier. Out of 300 suggestions it settled on "Peds," only to discover that the name was already being used. The "P" was replaced by a "K" (for kids) and Keds were born—25 million pairs in just one year. They soon became the nation's top-selling tennis sneak. Today, Keds and Pro-Keds are products of the Uniroyal Corporation, but sneak historians still think of them fondly as the National India Rubber Company shoe.

*Cover of the National India Rubber Company official history.*

In 1908, Marquis M. Converse was toiling away in a shack in Malden, Massachusetts, producing rubber overshoes. He called himself (and his handful of employees) the Converse Rubber Company. Nine years later, he could afford a new factory, and out of it came the best basketball shoe on the market—the Converse All-Star. "Connies" are still the slam-dunk champs, particularly in the New York area.

Ach, those Dassler brothers. They haven't spoken to each other since 1949. At one time, they jointly owned and operated the Dassler Sports Shoes Company of Herzogenaurach, Germany. Then war erupted, family relations were strained, and Adolf founded Adidas while Rudolph sired Puma. Today, Adidas is the largest sports shoemaker in the world, and Puma is the second largest in Europe. (In the late 1950's, desperate to overtake Adidas sales, Rudolph tried a new ploy: payola. He paid professional athletes to switch to Puma. But Adi liked the idea so much that he followed suit, and the companies continued growing at comparable rates.) At the 1968 Olympics in Mexico, the brothers waged an open bidding war. Amateur athletes, technically not allowed to accept money for endorsing a product, "found" thousand-dollar bills tucked in their sneakers by the daring Dasslers. The Olympic Committee screamed, the contestants got quite a bit richer and the brothers stalemated each other.

Courtesy Puma

*Rudi Dassler's place.*

# Skippies

Along Seventh Avenue, when a company copies a famous design, line for line, then renders it in a cheaper fabric, it's called a "knock-off." In the sneaker world, knock-offs are termed "skippies." They sell for half the price, carry no brand label and are usually available at chain discount stores. Skippies are not particularly well-made, but a lot of mothers buy them anyway—figuring their kids will outgrow them before they fall apart.

# Sneaker world map

**U.S.** feet wear out more than 220 million pairs of sneaks a year. Over half of them are imported. Sixty-five million pairs fly in from Taiwan, 31.4 million from South Korea, 3 million from Japan and 1.3 million from Hong Kong. The rest make their way here from Germany and South America, and if you're counting, it adds up to billions of dollars' worth of business.

Some American companies are not only major importers, but major underwriters of Oriental factories. Why? Simple economics. In the Far East, labor unions are unheard of and workers can be hired for a seven-day week, a fourteen-hour day, for only $7.

Other domestic companies feel the crunch, however, and in 1974 they won a hearing with the International Trade Commission, which decided imports were damaging the economy. After a second session of the Committee in 1977, the U.S. Government took steps to protect American shoe manufacturers by asking countries to restrict their exports.

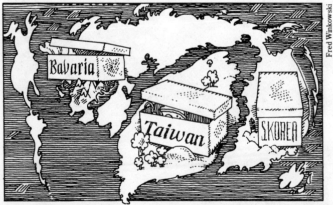

Fred Winkowski

Which country spawned what sneak? Most of the no-name sneaks ("skippies," to the trade) come from Korea, while West Germany birthed both Adidas and Puma, Japan created both Tiger and Pony, Brazil originated Cobra, France started Patrick, England manufactured Dunlop, Finland produced Gola, and the United States was responsible for Nike (out of Oregon), Etonic (from Massachusetts), Bata (from Maryland)—to name just a few points of origin.

# Label list

Adidas

New Balance

AMF Head

Bancroft (Tretorn)

Bata

Nike

Bauer

Braun

Brooks

Noel

Ours of America

Osaga

Pacific Trail Sportswear

Patrick

Patriot

Penn Athletic Products

Chris Craft

Cobra

PF

Pony

Converse

Dunlop

Eaton (Etonic)

E.B. Sport International
  (Lydiard)

Famolare Sport

Finalist

Foot Joy

Franklin (Jaclar)

Glen

Gola

Gold Seal Rubber

Hyde

Intermark

JSE Masters

Karhu

Kaepa

K-Swiss

Kidpower

LaCrosse

Lotto

Mitre

Pro Group

Puma

Rani Merona

Reebok

Saucony

Sebago

Sneak Slides of California

Soma

Specs

Spot-Bilt

Super Pro

Tempo

Tennis Togs

Thom McAn (Jox)

Tiger

Tred II

Uniroyal (Keds,
  Pro-Keds)

Van Doren

Weider

# Sneaker catalog

**Y**ou're ready for a new pair of sneakers. And you know *exactly* what you want. Then you look around the store and confusion sets in. There's just too much to choose from. (Adidas alone makes over 100 different styles.) To help you out, we've narrowed the field by picking our favorites from what's currently available.* Now if we only knew your size, we'd be in business.

## Running

*Prices are approximate.

**New Balance 320.** Rated the top training shoe by *Runner's World*. Sizes 3½AA—15EEEE. $30.

**Brooks Vantage 430.** "Racing Stud" sole, great for cross-country traction. Features "varus wedge" (⅛" extra padding at inner side of heel). $30.

**Nike LD-1000.** Extra wide "waffle" sole, nylon mesh upper. $35. For women, the Lady Waffle Trainer, $30.

**Adidas Formula 1.** "Spoiler" sole extension for maximum shock absorption and "catapult" effect. Geometrically patterned surface for super grip. $38.

**Puma Easy Rider.** Well-padded nylon training shoe. Sole studded with cones that dig in or absorb shock. $39. For women, the Joy Rider, $39.

**Nike Elite.** Rated top competition running shoe by *Runner's World*. Perfect for marathons. $34.

**Etonic Street Fighter.** Specially cushioned heel and ball of shoe. Abrasion-resistant outsole. $30. Women's version. $30.

**Adidas Nite Jogger.** Bright white "Cangoran" uppers. Trademark stripes and heel in red reflecting material (act like taillights). $30.

# Basketball

**Converse All-Star.** Best-selling basketball shoe in U.S. Available in high and low cuts. Black, white, maroon, purple, gold, green, orange, navy, red, light blue. Extra-large sizes too. High-tops, $19; low-tops, $15.

**Pro-Keds Royal.** Soles designed for durability on pavement. Available in high and low cuts. $15.

**Adidas Super Star.** Began trend towards leather. Tough, stitched-on sole. Available in high and low cuts. High-tops, $37; low-tops, $33.

# Tennis

**Patrick Competition.** From France. Also good for squash and other court sports. $30.

**Adidas Finalist.** Lace-to-toe canvas upper. Nubbed rubber sole. Absorbent terry cloth lining. $15. For women, the Monica, $15.

**Converse Chris Evert.** Candidate for world's most popular women's tennis shoe. Lightweight canvas upper. Herringbone-patterned rubber sole. Narrow and medium widths. $22.

**Adidas Stan Smith.** Perforated uppers. Polyurethane soles with herringbone tread. Fine for hard-court sports. $30.

# Fencing

**Adidas Fencing.** Resembles running flats. Rubber and suede protection on heel and toe. $30.

# Volleyball

**Tiger "Rotation."** Extra-low cut. Rubber and suede toe protection. $23.

# Hammer Throwing

**Puma International Hammer.** Designed especially for spinning motion. $68.

# Discus Throwing

**Puma Discus.** Emphasis on toe balance. Perfect for dirt or cinder track. $55.

# Boating

**Sperry Top-Sider.** Soft but tough leather uppers. Nonskid rubber soles. Ultimate no-socks, snob sneaker. $30.

# Wrestling

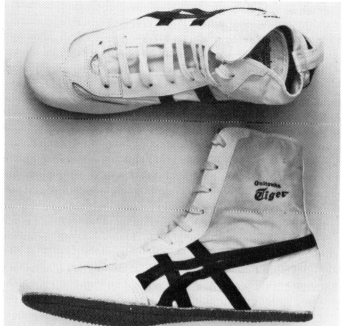

**Tiger Wrestling.** Highest cuts available. Lightweight nylon. Thin soles perfect for disco wear. $18.

Kate Simon

*As any clerk will tell you, we've omitted a few basic sneaks — such as the ones for javelin throwing, bicycling, parachute-jumping. But that doesn't mean they're not available. You have only to ask...*

# Sneak preview

**N**ot that anybody asked us, but we have a few ideas that we wouldn't mind seeing incorporated in sneakers. For example, The Wall Street Sneaker would have ticker tape instead of laces. All we need to put it on the board is venture capital. Interested? Then there's the Nudist's Sneaker. Dirt cheap to produce and one size fits all. Of course, in fairness not all our ideas have been smashing successes. To wit: the Ecology Sneaker (the lettuce wilted), the Bermuda Triangle Sneaker (it kept disappearing), the Skier's Sneak (it had to be waxed), the Ivy League Sneak (it flunked out), the Dog Walker's Sneaker (it nipped at the ankles), the Arab Sneak (not sheik).

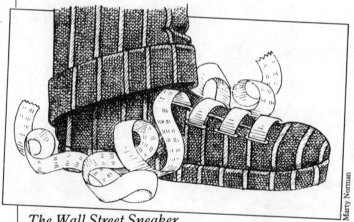

*The Wall Street Sneaker.*
Venture capital needed.

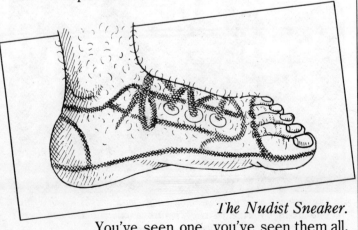

*The Nudist Sneaker.*
You've seen one, you've seen them all.

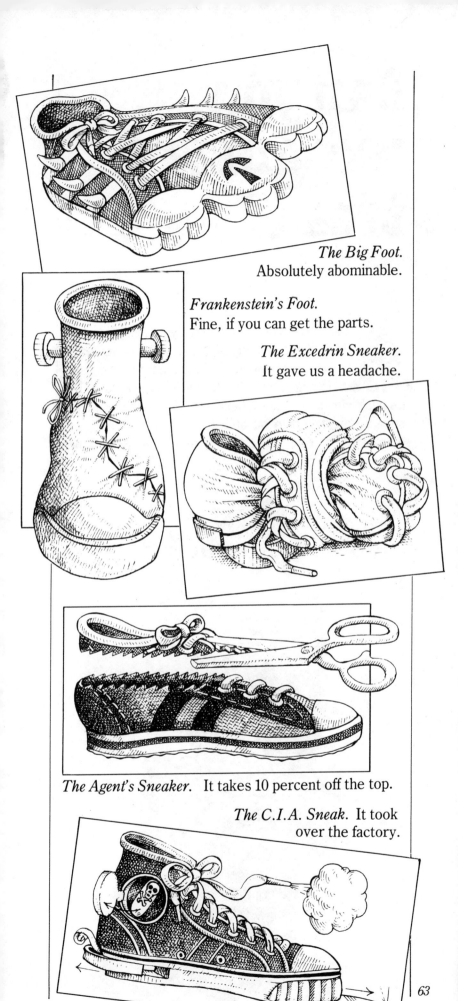

*The Big Foot.*
Absolutely abominable.

*Frankenstein's Foot.*
Fine, if you can get the parts.

*The Excedrin Sneaker.*
It gave us a headache.

*The Agent's Sneaker.* It takes 10 percent off the top.

*The C.I.A. Sneak.* It took over the factory.

# Can you recognize a tread?

**A**lmost everybody can identify an Adidas by its three diagonal stripes, a Converse by its star, a Nike by its check mark, a Tiger by its cross-hatching, a Pony by its two V's and a Puma by its back-curved stripe. Where's the fun in that? A real sneak expert should be able to spot the shoemaker even if he can't see the label or the logo—just by the treads.

1

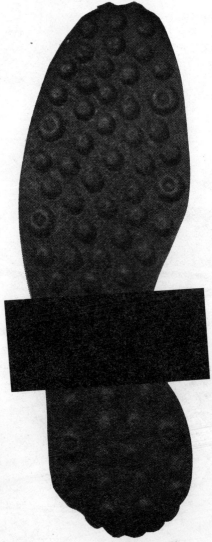

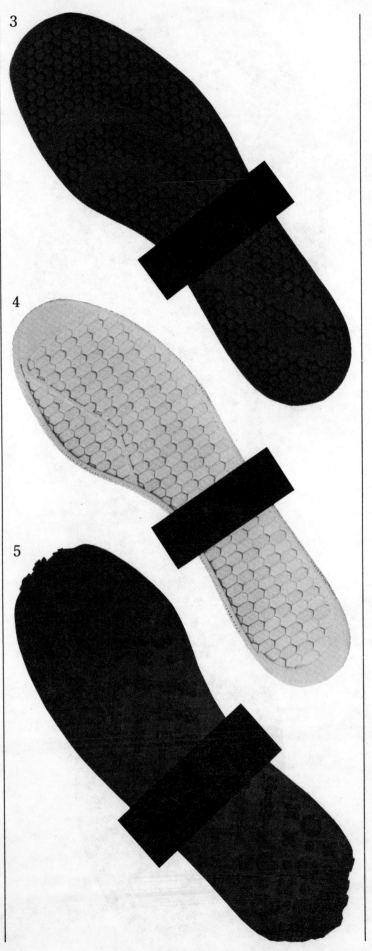

3

4

5

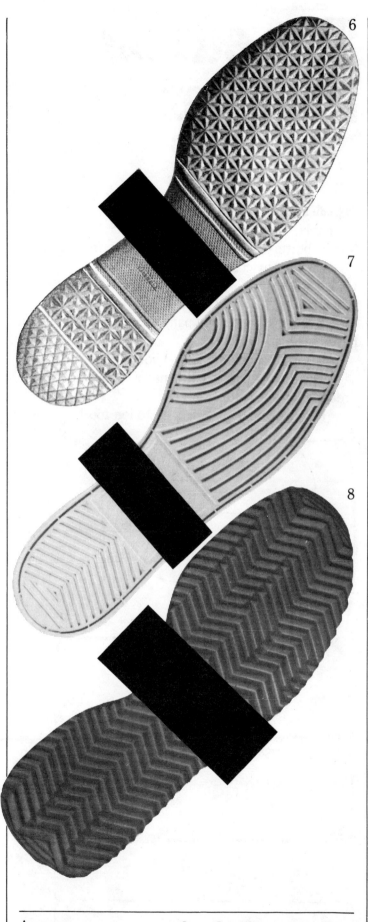

6

7

8

Answers:

1. Pony; 2. Pro-Keds; 3. Puma; 4. Patrick;
5. Tiger; 6. Keds; 7. Spalding; 8. Tiger

# The edible sneaker

**Ingredients:**

Cake mix, 1 box

Vanilla butter-cream frosting, 2 recipes (found on the
    back of any confectioners' sugar box)

Chocolate frosting, ½ recipe

**Procedure:**

Bake cake in oblong pan, 9″ x 13″ (larger, if you
have big feet).

Let cake cool for at least 1 hour.

Make two paper patterns of your feet (trace
around them—see diagram A).

Be sure you have a right and a left foot!

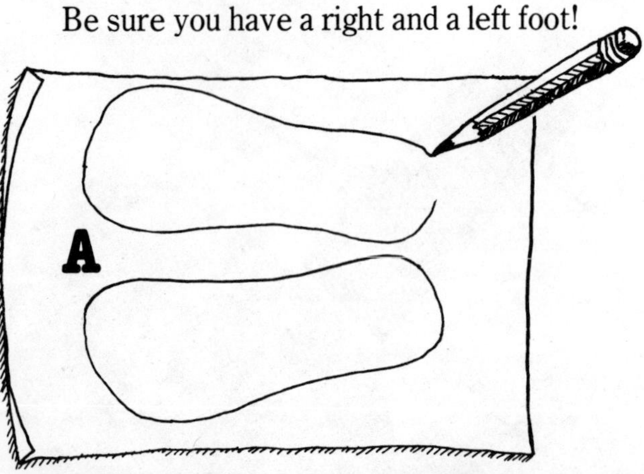

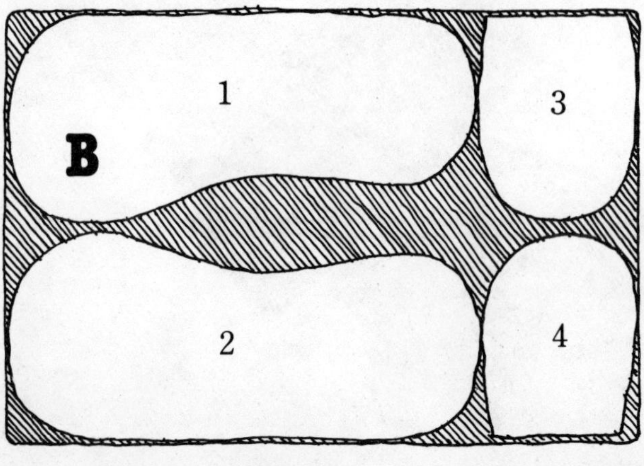

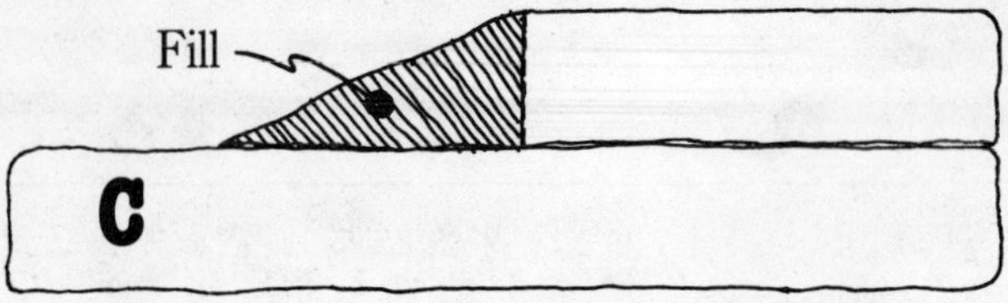

Place patterns on cake so that their toes rest against one edge.

Now back to the drawing board to trace only the heel portion of your feet.

Place heel patterns on cake, behind full-foot patterns (see diagram B).

Make frosting.

With sharp knife and steady hand, return to cake and cut out full-foot forms.

Transfer them to a 14″ x 18″ serving board covered with wax paper.

Frost them completely.

Cut out heel pieces and carefully transfer them to heel portions of frosted cake (making a double layer at back).

Use leftover scraps to fill in gaps between layers (see diagram C—think of them as arch supports).

If necessary, shave some of the cake (use a straight-edge) to give a smooth, angled line.

Frost top layer only on the outside.

Where a foot would enter the sneaker, frost with chocolate icing.

Outline tongue and edges with a No. 10 frosting cone. (Don't forget to indicate the sneaker seams.)

Make ripply lines on front of sneaker to indicate eyelets.

Again using a No. 10 cone, make the laces.

Write an appropriate message on the chocolate section (how about *John Smith, family All-Star*).

Serve, reminding diners that Walt Frazier was once presented with an identical cake—the handiwork of Creative Cakes' Stephanie Crookston.

# Sneaker specialty stores

*Fitting stools, Athlete's Foot.*

**T**wenty years ago, if you needed a new pair of sneakers, you went to a department store, or your neighborhood shoe store, or—for athlete-oriented brands—to a sporting goods store.

Now, because of the Sixties Sneaker Boom, there are stores that sell sneakers and almost nothing else. Probably the first of these was The Sneaker Shop, founded in 1963 in Bridgeport, Connecticut. At about the same time, Sneaker Circus, in Toledo, Ohio, began as a sort of charitable operation, selling low-cost factory close-outs and seconds; eventually, they expanded their stock to include more expensive lines such as Converse.

Athlete's Foot is the biggest chain of all-sneaker stores in operation today, with 131 branches in forty-four states. The great appeal of the chain is its huge selection for a wide variety of sports, as well as its high standard of service.

Principal competitor of Athlete's Foot is a chain called The Athletic Attic, which has forty-two stores, mainly in the South. The Attic concentrates on running, and two of its partners are giants in the field: Jimmy Carnes, former track coach of the University of Florida; and Marty Liquori, the world's top 5,000 meter runner, who also designs running shoes for Brooks. Both the Athletic Attic and the Athlete's Foot also sell accessories such as warm-up suits, shorts and socks.

The enormous success of these chains has not gone unnoticed by the big shoe companies, and now they're getting into the act, too. Kinney has initiated a chain of sneaker stores called The Footlocker, which sells Kinney's own sneakers as well as other popular national brands. And Thom McAn has moved in with Jox Stores, featuring their own Jox brand athletic shoes.

But if you think the sneaker store is a specialized concept, you ain't seen nothing yet—because the latest trend is the *women's* sneaker store. The Activist is a gigantic sporting goods store in Orange County, California, which sells only women's shoes. Pro-Women's Sports of Tucson, Arizona, is an even bigger operation, offering the best women's sports shoes while weeding out those models advertised as "men's or women's" but which do not in fact fit women's feet.

# sneaker anatomy

# Are sneaks bad for your feet?

|  | True | False |
|---|---|---|
| 1. If you wear sneaks in winter, you'll catch cold. | ☐ | ☐ |
| 2. Your feet get more tired in sneaks than in penny loafers. | ☐ | ☐ |
| 3. Sneaks make your feet smell. | ☐ | ☐ |
| 4. Sneaks give you flat feet. | ☐ | ☐ |
| 5. Sneaks don't let your feet "breathe." | ☐ | ☐ |
| 6. Always buy sneaks one size smaller than your regular shoes. | ☐ | ☐ |
| 7. Sneaks stretch your Achilles tendon. | ☐ | ☐ |
| 8. Sneaks make you pigeon-toed. | ☐ | ☐ |
| 9. Your feet will spread if you wear sneaks. | ☐ | ☐ |
| 10. Sneaks don't give your ankles enough support. | ☐ | ☐ |
| 11. If you wear sneaks, you'll catch athlete's foot. | ☐ | ☐ |
| 12. Sneaks cause bone spurs. | ☐ | ☐ |
| 13. Sneaks make your feet itch. | ☐ | ☐ |
| 14. If you put a toddler in sneaks, you'll stunt his foot growth. | ☐ | ☐ |
| 15. People who wear sneaks all the time can't keep their balance in ordinary shoes. | ☐ | ☐ |

Marty Norman

If you answered Yes to any of these questions, you've listened to too many rumors. None of the above is true.

# 26 bones of contention

**Y**our feet are probably better constructed than the Brooklyn Bridge. They contain (per foot) 19 muscles, 26 bones and 107 ligaments, all of which were issued to you in good working order. Before you take your leave—feet first—they'll have carried you a distance of 65,000 miles, which is roughly equivalent to ten round-trips from New York to L.A.

An ordinary pair of sneakers could hardly wreck such engineering marvels. That's your job, and don't think you're not up to it.

When you jog, for instance, you send 80 percent of your body's weight crashing down on your heels. Sure, your heel bone may give out—but not because it's genetically unsound. It was never designed to withstand *that* much pressure a half-hour a day, day in, day out.

You must also be a little more considerate of your metatarsals, since they're the most easily broken bones in your foot. (If a 200-pounder steps on them and says he's sorry, that won't do much good. While he's apologizing, they'll probably be lying there wrecked.) With the calcaneus, the metatarsals form your longitudinal arch. They should be supported from below with a steel shank and a substantial cushion, and from above with a flexible upper.

A nightly foot massage would be a blessing for your feet. Yes, you can use hand lotion.

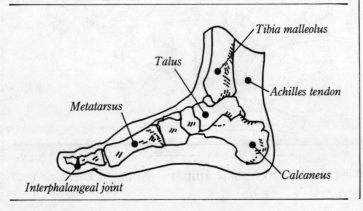

Tibia malleolus

Talus

Achilles tendon

Metatarsus

Calcaneus

Interphalangeal joint

# Exactly where is the metatarsal arch?

**W**hen you look at a wet footprint, it's the part that's missing.

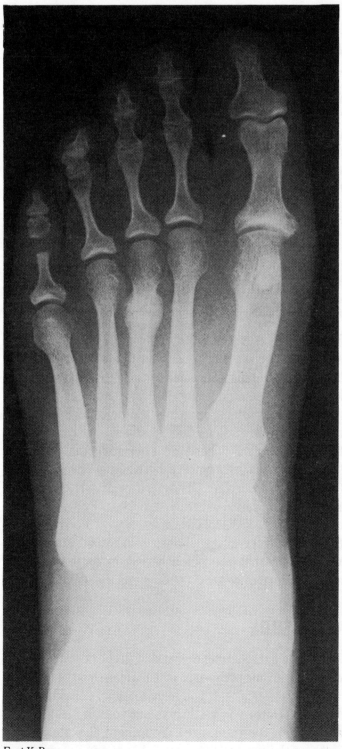

*Foot X-Ray.*

# Common ailments

## Athlete's foot

The itch could drive you crazy, and unfortunately this fungus infection is very difficult to cure. It lurks at the poolside or in the showers. No one is immune to it, but heavy perspirers and people whose toes are close together are perhaps most prone. If you should catch it, switch to porous footwear and stay scrupulously clean. There are two types: *T. rubrum* (chronic), which involves the entire sole of the foot, and *T. mentagrothytes* (acute), which flares up between the toes. Treat the acute form with Whitfield's ointment or cortisone, the chronic type with an antifungal drug such as Griseofulvin.

## Blisters

They're fun to squish, but restrain yourself. Doctors say the cause is acute trauma to the skin. In laymen's terms, this means your sneaker rubs. Blisters are collections of free fluid formed by your body as a barrier against the offending material. Sometimes a blister is caused not by friction, but by stress — psychological blisters, if you will. These are a by-product of excessive sweating and usually emerge between your toes and on the soles of your feet. They are clear white in color. Remember: *Never* puncture a blister. Put a Band-aid over it and let it disappear on its own. To prevent blisters, try better-fitting shoes; remove all soap when washing feet, dry meticulously and, in extreme cases, apply tincture of benzoin (it toughens the skin).

## Calluses

A callus is a thickening of the skin (hyperkeratosis). Its cause is chronic pressure, which means you bought the wrong-size sneaks. If you have a callus, consider using foot pads (after you've thrown out your ill-fitting shoes and bought the right size). You might also abrade the callus with pumice stone, available at any pharmacy.

# Corns

Medically speaking, the corn (clavus) is usually located over the interphalangeal joint, most frequently the fifth one. It's caused by outside pressure, again from badly fitting shoes, and can be helped by padding and unguents containing salicylic acids, i.e., Dr. Scholl's corn plaster. Sometimes it must be cut with a knife (excised) and the underlying bone shaved.

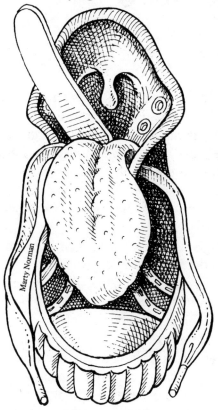

# How to tell if you've ruptured your Achilles tendon

**Y**ou'll hear a loud crack. This will be followed by unbelievable pain—as if you've just been smacked in the calf with a baseball bat. Why the calf, when the tendon is actually at the back of your heel? When it snaps, there's only one place for it to go — up. You also won't be able to stand on the toes of the afflicted foot.

Most often, ruptures happen to out-of-shape amateur athletes who try to get back in condition too fast—and too violently.

The only treatment is surgery.

If you've just *pulled* the tendon, however, you can make it better by keeping your weight off your feet. Go to bed.

# The podiatrists' report

**M**r Sneekers, a Division of the Mitsubishi International Corporation, conducted a national survey on sneaker habits in the mid-1960's. *Boot and Shoe Recorder* magazine published the results. They indicated that:

Sixty percent of the doctors surveyed wore sneakers themselves, but only for specific activities and short periods of time.

Eighty-seven percent of their kids wore sneaks, but only under their strict supervision.

Fifty-three percent had used sneakers therapeutically for patients recovering from surgery and those with heel problems, temporary infections or swellings.

Only 11 percent objected to sneakers. Their reasons: Low-cuts didn't provide enough support for growing feet; if worn all day, sneaks often produced foot strain; severe cases of weak feet got worse; sneaker-wearing caused excessive perspiration, which in turn caused corns, calluses, skin infections, blisters and warts.

More recently, in *Science Digest* magazine, Dr. Rob Roy MacGregor, chief of podiatry at Boston's New England Deaconess Hospital, was interviewed on the sneaks-give-no-support issue. "Hogwash," he

## The convalescent sneaker

**H**igh-tops are sometimes therapeutic. At Philadelphia's Thomas Jefferson University Hospital, the doctor of a seventy-nine-year-old woman patient recommended that she wear them while her feet were in traction. Without them, he felt, her feet would have had no support and would have fallen forward, further weakening her ankles and shortening her calf muscles.

said. "[It's] a concept I categorically reject, since the foot has its own built-in support system. Kids don't get tired wearing sneakers, but that fat, indolent, hypertensive adult who runs around in his sneakers on weekends is going to have a lot of problems. That's mainly because he *is* fat and indolent and hypertensive and he has a lousy musculo-skeletal system. I don't think we should blame the sneaker."

In *On Your Feet,* Elizabeth H. Roberts, D.P.M., discussed the problem of "tennis toe," a condition caused by some of the newer sneaker brands because "they provide such excellent traction that the foot, in sudden stops, is jammed against the front of the shoe, injuring the nails of the first and second toe." She assigns the blame for it to "European designed tennis shoes ....They are made on longer, narrower lasts than American tennis shoes, causing greater crowding of the toes." This information was provided to her by Dr. H.V. Roth, an expert in the treatment of "tennis toe."

The American Medical Association and the American Podiatry Association take no official position on the sneaker. The National Foot Council, however, maintains that sneakers with built-in supports "can be worn safely for recreational footwear."

# Sneaker guilt

**M**om, the doctor.

According to her, sneaks will give you flat feet, fat feet, swollen ankles, bulbous heels, ingrown toenails, even hangnails.

And if all that doesn't stop you, she brings out her heavy artillery: *You will not leave the house until you have changed shoes!*

Except for the last, all her threats are meaningless. There is not one shred of scientific proof connecting sneaks with bad feet.

It's all in Mom's head.

Still, such is the power of mothers that the guilt lingers on. Most of us, deep down, believe we're getting away with something when we wear our sneaks. And we're not entirely convinced that our feet won't rot away within the hour.

Let it be said once and for all: No such thing will happen. If you mother's taste doesn't run to sneaks, fine; she doesn't have to wear them. But she has no right to intimidate you with false information.

Isn't it time you stood up to her?

# If the shoe fits...

**S**hoe "sizes" were created during the reign of King Edward II of England. The longest man's foot (at that time) was equal to the length of 39 barleycorns in a row. This became "size" 13. If a foot reached one barleycorn less, it was deemed a 12; two less, an 11; and so on. Not very scientific, was it?

These days, size is measured by two remarkably accurate devices: the Ritz stick and the Brannock Metal Fitting Tray. You've probably seen both of them in various shoe stores. It would pay you well to insist that the clerk use them. A jaunty "I wear a 6, don't bother with that thing—I'm in a rush" is ridiculous. You wouldn't wear a 6 in every shoe. And you won't stay a 6 all your life. (For one thing, if you've gained weight, your feet may have gone up a size.) Also, shoes are made on different lasts. Some of them are roomier than others. In which case, you'll only need a 5.

The best time to get fitted for a sneak is in the late afternoon. That's when your feet are the biggest, having been tramped on all day. Measure both of them and get sneaks to fit the larger one (you can always put a heel cusion or an inner sole in the other one). Once the sneaks are on, stand up. Your feet are slightly longer and wider with weight on them. Try on both shoes—to make sure what's right for the right one is right for the left.

Now, about that wiggling-your-toes syndrome.

## Lasts

**R**egular shoes come in widths, but most sneaks don't. You have to take what they give you and make do. People with wide feet should investigate Puma (which is built on almost a triple E last) or New Balance (a D last). Those with very narrow feet should try on a Nike or an Adidas. Of course, if you fall in between, you can start with any of the brands you like.

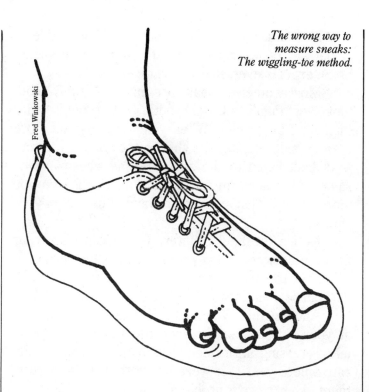

Fred Winkowski

Most people think if they can wiggle, the sneak fits. No such thing. Your toes might have plenty of room and the shoe might still be too small for you. Size is determined by arch length—the measurement from the heel to the ball of your foot—not by heel-to-toe length. If the ball of your foot doesn't coincide with that of the shoe, try another size. Maybe even another brand.

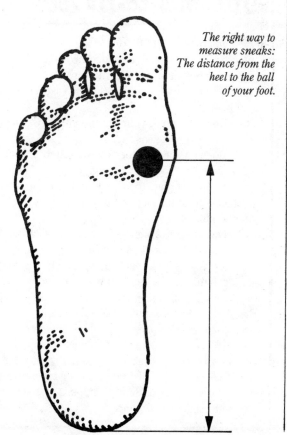

*The right way to measure sneaks: The distance from the heel to the ball of your foot.*

Fred Winkowski

Insofar as your toes are concerned, allow at least ¼" leeway between them and the top of your sneak. Some experts even advise ½" grace.

Most women's sneaks are made to fit a B-width foot; most men's, a C to D width. If your foot is wider than that, be careful. When your laces extend more than ½" side to side, the shoe is too narrow for you. And don't listen to the sweet-talking salesman who says, "Aw, lace 'em up lace-to-toe; that'll give you more room." That's one good way to bust out of your shoes.

Notice the heel counter. If you can stick your finger in-between it and your foot, the shoe doesn't fit right. It's too loose. We've all heard of people "walking" out of their shoes. This is one reason they do.

Another thing you might do is take a careful look at your old sneaks. Examine them for worn spots, fabric creasing and incidental lumps. These things indicate where your feet were trying to make an adjustment. They're your problem areas.

Always remember that you're getting the shoe because you like your comfort. Don't settle for anything less.

# Difficult-to-fit feet

If you have any of the following foot abnormalities, you may have trouble wearing sneaks (or any other mass-produced shoe, for that matter).

Do you have a bunion (hallux valgus)? A sneak may aggravate it.

Does the tip of your big toe jut out (hallux varus)? A sneak may press against it.

Does one of your toes overlap another (hammertoe)? A sneak may not be deep enough for you.

Do any of your toes stick up in the air rather than lie flat (cock-up deformity)? A sneak may be too shallow for your comfort.

Do you have a higher-than-normal arch (pes cavus)? A sneak may not be wide enough for you.

Do you have flat feet (pes planus)? Sneaks with built-in arches may make you feel worse if they happen to fall in the wrong place. Sneaks, however, will not *cause* flat feet. Blame heredity (or a disease that causes severe muscle imbalance, such as polio). The most severe form of flat feet is called "calcaneovalgua foot," and it means you have absolutely no longitudinal arch at all so that your weight rests on the inner edge of your foot and your big toe. If this is the case, try sneaks with leather uppers as they *will* provide you with maximum support.

# The Kaepa double vamp

**I**f you have a high instep or narrow heels or wide feet, or if you've just been plain uncomfortable in sneakers for no reason you can put your finger on, try the Kaepa. It looks weird, but it works.

The Kaepa is the brainchild of tennis buff Tom Adams. He broke a lace during a match, called time-out and knotted the lace—but not in the usual way. He tied the ends separately, as if the shoe had two sets of laces. That felt so good, he purposely broke the lace on his other shoe and redid that one, too. Later, after the match (we don't know if he won or not), he took a pair of scissors to the vamps of his shoes. Now he had two sets of laces and two vamps, per shoe. And the shoes did seem to fit better. The top vamp adjusted one way for the foot's forward motion, the bottom vamp adjusted another way for its side-to-side movement.

Shortly thereafter, he went into production, and in 1975 twenty thousand Kaepas (named for his daughters, Mikaela and Paula) went on sale.

The shoes come in leather (about $30) or canvas (about $20) and are virtually revolutionizing the sneaker industry. If you'd like to try a pair, contact Kaepa, Inc., 10203 IH 35 North, San Antonio, Texas 78233.

# The anti-sneaker crusade

In 1950, sneakers accounted for a 5 percent share of the total shoe market. In 1957, 10 percent. In 1962, 20 percent. Then the leather industry decided to strike back — after all, billions of dollars were at stake — and mounted an intensive anti-sneaker campaign.

They focused on health questions. An ad in *Parents'* magazine advised, "Madam, only leather shoes assure your child proper support, correct fit and protection." Clearly, it was also designed to promote fear of social embarrassment: its leather shoe gleamed; its sneaker was half destroyed.

The Leather Industry Association released a five-minute cartoon to television stations. It told kids that sneakers were "out" and leathers "in." It mentioned health hazards as well, and was presented free to 5,000 junior and senior high school hygiene classes.

And they launched a massive publicity drive, resulting in newspaper headlines that screamed SNEAKERS FADE FROM FASHION and TEENS SHED SNEAKERS in such widely read papers as the *News* and the *Christian Science Monitor*.

Anti-sneaker ads appeared in *Seventeen* magazine, and a nationally syndicated beauty columnist warned parents that "rubber soled sneakers give growing feet no support." *No support* was the anti-sneaker catch phrase, even though the foot branch of the medical profession was by no means united on whether or not feet needed support. (Besides, sneaks had been on the market since 1939 with both heel and arch supports.)

The campaign, overall, was a dud. Today, the sneaker market accounts for 50 percent of the shoes sold in the United States—although, to be sure, some of the sneaks are sporting leather uppers and trim.

# sneaker game plan

# Sneaker sports

If the most strenuous exercise you do is clip the leash to the dog and walk to the corner, you don't need a true athletic shoe. An ordinary sneaker will do. Your feet aren't going to be in them long enough to suffer much damage.

But let's say you've decided to start the morning with ten minutes of Royal Canadian Air Force exercises. Or you've signed up for a three-times-a-week shape-up program at the local health club. Now you need something more sophisticated than a basic sneak, which is nothing more than a flimsy bit of canvas stuck to a chunk of rubber.

The tendency, of course, is to listen to that little voice in the back of your head that says, "Why invest in really good shoes when chances are you'll drop out of this health routine before very long?" The road to physical fitness is littered with people whose good intentions lasted only the length of time it took them to finish the magazine article on the newest "in" sport.

So, in the interests of economy and your short attention span, you attempt to exercise in whatever shoes are handy. The first ones you find in the back of

*The Tiger fencing sneak has a slightly elevated and rounded heel.*

© Thomas Hopker

> **"** It's so comfortable wearing sneakers. You don't have to kick them off, you can sit in them for hours. **"**
>
> **Billy "White Shoes" Johnson,** All-Star kick return specialist, Houston Oilers

Skateboarding demands two things:
courage and a helmet.
A sturdy pair of sneaks
is also suggested.

United Press International

the closet are "it." Never mind that these shoes were bought twenty pounds ago, that they provide absolutely no support, that — even worse — they'd been relegated to the closet because they were never comfortable anyway.

An hour in shoes of this type would tire (and pain) even Bruce Jenner. Certainly, if you're flabby and if your idea of a good stretching regime has been to reach across the front seat of the car to open the window on the far side, you're not going to find calesthenics a snap —no matter how mild they are. You *are* going to get tired. But by wearing the wrong shoes you're aggravating the problem. The rule of thumb is: The less exercise you're used to, the more you need a well-built pair of sneaks, ones designed for your specific activity. That's what the shoe clerk is getting at when he asks what sport you play and steers you over to the more expensive ones in the line. (Most people think he's only trying to hustle them. Not true.)

Plan on spending about $30 for a new pair of sneaks. You need to. Cheaper ones won't have enough "comfort" features for your wobbly legs. For example, when was the last time you bought gym shoes? Were they padded? Inexpensive sneaks usually aren't and that's the bane of the amateur athlete. It wears him out.

*As yet, no one has made a sneaker specifically for unicycling. There are, however, special bike sneaks, dating from the late 30's (Keds).*

Now let's consider the wrong-shoe-for-the-wrong-sport syndrome. Sure you can wear jogging shoes to play tennis in. But it's a little like trying to return Connors' serve with a badminton racket. You may be able to do it, but how long do you think that racket will last? And don't you think you're going to have to work twice as hard to compensate for its weakness? The same applies with sneaks. Running shoes are built for forward movement; tennis shoes, for lateral ones. Your poor feet will be run ragged if you try to interchange them. You may develop "tennis toe" or "jogger's knee," and ache so much you decide to give up the game in favor of watching it on TV.

The solution, then, is to wear a basketball shoe for basketball, a skateboard shoe for skateboarding. Not so strange, really. You wouldn't try to make a hoop with a shuttlecock, anymore than you'd attempt to play a set on a cinder track. And sneaks are no less important to the game's success than the proper ball and the proper arena.

Sneakers have been designed for almost every sport: tennis, jogging, racing, boating, wrestling, fencing, parachute jumping, hammer throwing, discus throwing, basketball, racket ball, squash, skateboarding, even weightlifting. First pick out your game, then dress for it. With sneaks that give you ample support.

You may discover you have more stamina than you thought.

*Americans are not the only ones enamored of sneakers. Here, a Scot wears them to compete in, midst the heather on the field. Have you ever heard sneaker pronounced with a brogue? It's simple. All you do is burr your rrrrrrs.*

*You're never too young, or too old, to wear sneaks and get a healthy dose of physical exercise everyday. Some sports you might like to choose from: Baseball, Field Hockey, Softball, Frisbee, Tumbling, Handball, Volleyball, Javelin throwing, Skateboarding, and just plain old-fashioned walking.*

# Million dollar feet

**T**here are eight seconds left. Philadelphia inbounds the ball to Doctor J, who dribbles once, then goes up for the shot. Did you see the winning basket? If you were watching on TV, maybe not. All right, let's watch the instant replay. Erving grabs the ball, bounces it, enters the air. So far, so good. The action's clear. But now, instead of a close-up of the hoop, the screen's all feet—Doctor J's feet, seemingly suspended in midair. Notice anything special about them? Like what kind of sneaks are on them? That's what the Converse folks are banking on. A free plug.

Of course, there's a catch to the "free" part. Converse (and Pro-Keds, Adidas, Puma, Bata and just about everyone who makes athletic equipment) pay the pros large sums of money to run, leap, lunge, jump, throw, toss, serve, volley and cross the finish line in their sneakers.

Good sports don't come cheap. Their attitude is: If you want me, meet my price. Usually, the manufacturers do. They want that TV exposure. They want you to see your heroes in their shoes. And then maybe, just maybe, the next time you go to buy a new pair, you'll switch to their brand.

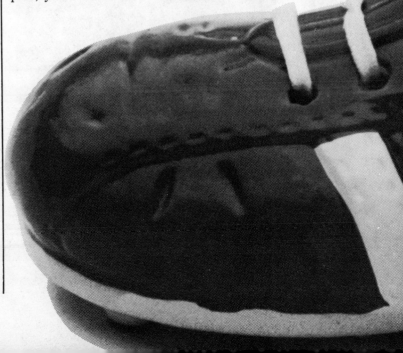

How profitable is the practice? Very. For rookies in the NBA, the going rate for endorsements is $1,000. Bona fide superstars like Doctor J pull down much more—as much as $35,000. But tennis stars are best paid of all. Rumor has it that Nastase received a cool million for signing his name on the dotted line. What did he have to do in exchange? Swear he wouldn't switch to Brand X for the life of the contract.

Some companies won't pay the pros, but they'll practically swamp them with "freebies." All the sneaks they can wear (some athletes have so many they could open up their own shoe store); gym bags, sweatsuits, T-shirts; even in some cases, uniforms.

Does seeing a star in a certain sneak affect sales? Pro-Keds and Converse, according to an article in *The Wall Street Journal,* think so. They believe celebrity endorsements are winning them a larger share of the urban market than they would otherwise reach.

But you have to wonder if the plan isn't backfiring —if the companies aren't giving out more than they're getting back. Stan Smith, who has an arrangement with Adidas which includes a "Stan Smith" sneak complete with his picture on it (he looks a little like Teddy

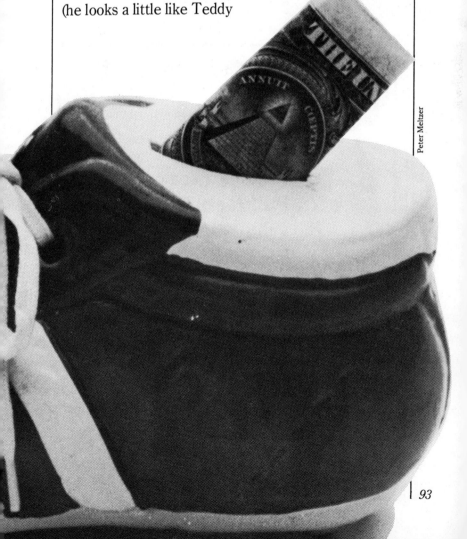

Peter Meltzer

Roosevelt), recalls a flight from Nairobi when "the maintenance men came on the plane and one of them looked like he couldn't afford three meals a day. But he had on *my* shoes. With no shoelaces."

Bob Cousy, on the other hand, remembers that the Randolph Shoe Company sold 1.4 million pairs of the Cousy sneak, and it retailed for $7.95. They claim, perhaps rightly, that they did it on the strength of his name.

What it all boils down to is this: the fifteen- to seventeen-year old kids, who buy most of the sneaks, are impressionable. They believe if they wear what their idol wears, they'll play just that much better. So they tend to look for their hero's shoes when they're out shopping around.

If you associate certain players with certain brand names, and this influences you when you buy your shoes, the manufacturer considers he's made a good investment. And he'll continue backing the pros (and sponsoring sporting events and providing free shoes to Olympic contestants). In a sense, you could say you're a victim of advertising.

And the wealthy pros certainly aren't complaining.

---

# Half-time entertainment

Each of the following pros has received a hefty sum for endorsing a certain sneaker line. Can you name their sponsor? On your mark, get set, go...

1. **Virginia Wade**
2. **Billie Jean King**
3. **John Newcombe**
4. **Ilie Nastase**
5. **Chris Evert**
6. **Tom Seaver**
7. **Bruce Jenner**
8. **Bob McAdoo**
9. **Walt Frazier**
10. **Elvin Hayes**

---

*Answers:* 1. Pro-Keds; 2. Adidas; 3. Lotto; 4. Adidas; 5. Converse; 6. Cobra; 7. Brown Shoes; 8. Pony; 9. Puma; 10. Nike

94

# The ideal basketball shoe

**G**iven the amount of time a basketball shoe spends in the classroom and the study hall, it ought to be absolutely brilliant by now. The basketball shoe fetish begins in about the seventh grade, then continues through graduation or the nineteenth year—whichever comes first. It is impossible to walk through a schoolyard in the continental U.S.A. and not find a pair.

No one has ever documented its fascination. All we know is, it's there. And we're willing to make a few educated guesses as to why. First of all, young teenagers are very impressionable. They're relentless in their pursuit of idols. Girls tend to find their heroes among rock stars; boys, among sports stars. Now, if you were looking for a hero, a magical figure to pin all your hopes on, who better than a seven-foot giant—a man who can defy gravity and earn buckets of money for it? Right, a basketball star. The kids are trying to fill their shoes. (Which will take some doing. Average size in the NBA is 14. Bob Lanier gets honors with a 22.)

*John Havlicek's birthday sneaks.*

United Press International

*Ever wonder what a pro's locker looks like? This one belonged to Hondo, Celtic team captain. If you look carefully, you may notice that the toiletry items on the shelf are lined up in the order in which they are to be used. A very tidy man, is Hondo.*

Doctors, mothers, teachers and most concerned adults have told the kids that basketball shoes are not good for their feet. Sure, they're fine if they get playing time, but they weren't meant to be walked in, to be used as an all-purpose shoe. The kids won't listen. To them a basketball shoe is more a state of mind than a "real" shoe. It makes a statement. Listen. You can't argue with feelings, no matter how much you may want to.

The truth is, basketball shoes are built on a pivot principle. They were designed for lateral movement, which is the exact opposite of what kids need to walk them down the hall corridors. But try to convince them of that.

---

# Taping an ankle

**A**nkle taping goes back to 1863, when a Civil War surgeon by the name of Gibney sent Union soldiers into action wrapped up with basket-weave bandages.

Celtic trainer Frank Challant boasts that he can do an ankle in eighteen seconds flat. He estimates it costs the club $7,500 a year to keep him supplied with pads, lubricants and the tape itself. That averages out to $5 a day per man.

Many teams, like the Celtics, fine a player if he goes into a game without his ankle taped and then sprains it.

*Frank Challant's procedure:*
Swab the foot with Vaseline.

Put a felt pad (approximately 1½" x 3") under the spot where the laces hit and another under the Achilles area.

Place a styrofoam-type underpad over the Achilles pad.

Now anchor these pads to the foot with at least two strips of tape (called "stirrups"), possibly as many as six—it depends on the size of the ankle.

The first stirrup begins at the base of the calf and extends to just below the big toe. It goes under the heel, not around, so you can rotate it.

The second stirrup does the same thing, but you start it in the opposite direction. If strip No. 1 began the outside of the foot (as it should have), strip No. 2 begins on the inside.

Wind the tape so that each revolution overlaps the one just before it. Be careful you don't cut off your circulation.

Now close the procedure by putting several short strips over the tape ends. Make them about 3" long.

Over all this go your socks. (The Celtics wear as many as three on each foot.)

If you're going to tape your ankles every time you play basketball, tape them before you go buy your sneaks. It could make a difference in your shoe size.

Most pros don't wear their basketball shoes off court. One exception, however, is Kevin Stacum, who likes to pair them with a blue velvet suit when he goes disco hopping.

On average, the pros wear out twenty to forty pairs per season. (Kids outdo them as far as longevity is concerned.) John Havlicek, recently retired captain of the Boston Celtics, says it's not the soles that wear out, it's the uppers. They lose their shape. Most pros favor leather uppers because of their strength and staying power, but some have to forgo it for canvas (which is less durable) because of foot injuries. For example, JoJo White has difficulties with his uppers because of bone spurs. His shoes are built up with special cushions, so they don't press on his feet. Dave Bing cuts a large hole in his sneaker, over his big toe, to accommodate an old injury. Even Hondo had trouble now and then, and his constant complaint was about uppers that stretched and bunched. And rubbed. Also,

Wide World Photos

*You hear a lot of talk about a "pro last," implying that the NBA stars wear different sneakers from yours. No such thing. The only discrepancy is size —theirs are made bigger.*

**66** I wear a dainty thirteen. **99**

**Bob Cousy,** former Celtic

*David Craig, Indiana Pacers' trainer, has known of cases in which a player switched his sneaks three times during one game. Not that there was anything wrong with them. But the pro had promised several manufacturers he'd appear in their designs, and he had to keep changing sneaks to keep all his sponsors happy.*

many pros bulge their uppers because they wear as many as four pairs of socks under them.

Hardwood floors, however, are not particularly lethal to sneaks. After a while, the tread markings may wear down (the same way a tire's tread does), causing you to slip and skid, but in general you can count on the sole to outlast the rest of the shoe. A flat sole is vital for balance and stability. Those with a crisscross pattern seem to work best. At the Athlete's Foot, they sell basketball sneaks with one kind of sole for indoor courts and one kind for outdoor. School kids might look into the latter.

One thing both pros and amateurs can agree on is high-tops. Every basketball sneak should have them, even those designed for girls. (They're just starting to feature them for women.) Kids like them because they look neat. Pros like them because they appreciate that extra ankle support when they're jumping, twisting, clogging the middle and, in the case of Monroe, doing that "Earl the Pearl Magic Show." Also, high-tops impede swelling, should you happen to get stepped on— which is an occupational hazard.

A good basketball shoe will cost about $25 and have a solid arch support, a wood-gripping sole and (usually) the Converse or Adidas logo. Other recommended brands are Pony, Puma and Cross-Court.

Now, if you could just remember to wear them on the basketball court, and not on the way to and from the gym, your feet would be a lot better off.

# NBA scorecard

| Team | Player | Sneaker |
|------|--------|---------|
| *Atlanta Hawks* | John Drew | Nike |
|  | Tree Rollins | Converse |
| *Boston Celtics* | Dave Cowens | Tigers |
|  | Curtis Rowe | Bata |
|  | Kevin Stacum | Converse |
|  | Kermit Washington | Adidas |
|  | JoJo White | Pro-Keds |
| *Buffalo Braves* | Nate Archibald | Pro-Keds |
|  | Bill Willoughby | Pony |
| *Chicago Bulls* | Artis Gilmore | Adidas |
|  | Norm VanLear | Pony |
| *Cleveland Cavaliers* | Austin Carr | Nike |
|  | Foots Walker | Nike |
| *Denver Nuggets* | Dave Thompson | Custom DT's |
|  | Bobby Wilkinson | Pony |
| *Detroit Pistons* | Bob Lanier | Converse |
|  | Ralph Simpson | Pony |
| *Golden State Warriors* | Ray Barry | Adidas |
|  | Charles Dudley | Pony |
| *Houston Rockets* | Kevin Kunnert | Pony |
| *Indiana Pacers* | Mike Bantom | Bata |
|  | James Edwards | Adidas |
|  | Rickey Sobers | Bata |
| *Kansas City Kings* | Richard Washington | Adidas |
|  | Lucius Allen | Nike |
| *Los Angeles Lakers* | Kareem Abdul Jabbar | Adidas |
|  | Jamal Wilkes | Bata |
| *Milwaukee Bucks* | Ernie Grunfeld | Nike |
|  | Marques Johnson | Pony |
| *New Jersey Nets* | Van Breda Kopf | Pony |
| *New Orleans Jazz* | Gus Bailey | Pony |
|  | Joe Meriweather | Pony |
| *New York Knicks* | Toby Knight | Pony |
|  | Earl Monroe | Pony |
| *Philadelphia 76ers* | Lloyd Free | Pony |
|  | Dr. J. | Pro-Keds |
| *Phoenix Suns* | Lloyd Neal | Nike |
|  | Paul Westphal | Pony |
| *Portland Trailblazers* | Corky Calhoun | Pony |
|  | Bill Walton | Adidas |
| *San Antonio Spurs* | Mike Gale | Converse |
|  | Billy Paultz | Adidas |
| *Seattle Supersonics* | Paul Silas | Pony |
| *Washington Bullets* | Joe Pace | Pony |
|  | Elvin Hayes | Nike |

# The best running shoe

**G**ood morning. Ready to start the day with a quick jog around the block? If you hurry, you'll find someone to keep you company. Over 10 percent of America is out there ahead of you, dodging dogs that snap at their heels, traffic that cuts them off at the corner — and other joggers, who weave in and out as if the park were a giant (but flat) slalom run.

Jogging, so it would seem, is quickly replacing baseball as the national pastime. And the more popular it gets, the more mysterious it becomes. According to all the latest magazine articles, it's a lot more complicated than putting one foot in front of the other and starting your motor. You have to worry about shin splints, jogger's knee, heel drift and your toe-off point. You must take into consideration your body weight, your hamstring stretch, your muscle balance. And once you've mastered your own physical peculiarities, you have to start in on the earth's. Is the terrain banked, for instance? Is it hard or soft, fast or slow, slippery, muddy or totally non-giving?

Quite obviously, a simple sneak isn't equal to jogging shenanigans. You need a masterfully constructed shoe, a veritable engineering triumph. Which the sneaker industry will be happy to supply you with.

*The start of the twenty-six mile New York Marathon.*

Jogging shoes invariably look like they were put together by Dr. Frankenstein. Their soles reach up from the floor, enveloping the heel with a mass of studs, waffles, dimples, nubs and other variations on the rubber cleat theme. Perhaps the most popular innovation is the "ripple" sole, which experts think all beginning joggers should have. In 1975, Nancy Lu Conrad, a podiatrist from Circleville, Ohio, conducted tests which pitted the ripple sole against tennis shoes and running shoes without ripples. She found that all of her testees felt more sure-footed in the ripples, that they had begun "to look forward automatically to the sessions with the ripple sole shoes." Two-thirds of the test group even announced that they planned to switch to ripple soles for running on a full-time basis.

Other reports from the medical front have indicated that the composition of the sole material is extremely important. For Sunday joggers—indeed, even for marathon runners — polyurethane is too hard a substance. It has little shock absorbency. Gum rubbers and gum rubbers plus carbons are preferred. (Shock absorbency is crucial. When you jog, according to *Science Digest,* you take "about 1700 strides per mile, [and] 80 percent of the body's weight comes down on a few square inches of heel." The aim of a shoe is to remove that impact from the foot, to let the shoe absorb it instead.)

*Science Digest* maintains that the best running shoes will incorporate the following features: They will have a *flared heel.* Flared heels give you more space to land on, which lessens the stress on the foot. Between the sole and the heel counter, they'll have a *wedge.* A wedge is a layer of cushioning (think of it as a thin strip of icing between two layers of cake). This wedge should stop just short of the ball of the foot—taper off to it. Again, it provides needed cushioning for sensitive feet. The heel itself should be elevated. An *elevated heel* protects the Achilles tendon. (Most of us have shortened Achilles tendons, and the elevation makes us more comfortable. Running shoes also need a *firmly*

> **66** I have a lot. Eight or nine pairs. I get them wherever I go. It's kind of a stimulant. I can be really down, and buy a new outfit to train, and believe it or not, it makes a world of difference. Sneakers are critical for a bodybuilder. Do you want to see my feet? **99**
>
> **Steve Davis,** Mr. World

# On the drawing board

"**A**ll runners have things they'd like to see done to shoes, but they have to be tempered by the limits of the shoe factory and by what is humanly possible. Sometimes, something crazy will end up on a shoe. For instance, I was looking at a belt sander with carborundum coating that's used for sanding down the shoes, and I thought this would be good to put on the back of a track spike for better traction. We tried it out and gave the new design to pole vaulters and runners. They all loved it. A much better gripping surface. And we have an inner sole that forms to your foot after you've worn it a while, and that was originally used to make hip pads and shoulder pads for football players. Some rubber in running shoes was designed for the astronauts. Every time I think there's nothing left to experiment with, something comes up. I don't know where it's going to stop."

**Marty Liquori** World Champion Runner (5,000 meters); Brooks Shoe Designer

---

*padded heel counter.* (We mentioned "heel drift" a moment ago. A rigid heel collar "locks" the heel in, keeps it from jiggling. The less it moves, the less likely you are to rub it raw and develop painful blisters.) A running shoe also needs a *rounded toe box.* Take a look at your naked feet. Is your second toe longer than your big toe? That gives you something in common with 40 percent of the population. A rounded toe box will give both toes ample room. This means you won't be jam-

*Kathy Miller of Syracuse, New York, entered the 1972 Boston Marathon in a form-fitting body stocking, a cotton mini-tunic and a pair of neatly polished running shoes. She momentarily broke stride between Hopkington and Boston to rearrange her hair.*

ming them against the sneak edge every time you step down, which is the chief cause of toe blood blisters. The final requirement for jogging shoes is that they have *flexibility*. There's a simple test for it. Take the shoe in one hand and try to bend it toward you, at the ball. If it doesn't move, forget it. This is the shoe's toe-off point. It's where your foot always bends. If the shoe won't conform to your foot, you'll find yourself in deep trouble.

In an effort to make running shoes lighter, many manufacturers have skimped on the shoe cushioning. Try to find a shoe that has been lavished with it. And the heavier you are, the more padding you'll need. In other words, a 100-pound girl can do with far less than a 200-pound man. The lightness of the shoe itself is a much-debated issue. On average, a running shoe weighs twelve ounces; a competition shoe, about seven ounces. You ought to be able to handle that.

Running shoes can have three different kinds of uppers: nylon, nylon mesh, leather. Nylon is the best-seller. The nylon mesh has a serious drawback in that it tends to make the feet cold (the wind whips right through the mesh). Leather, of course, provides the most support for the foot, but it does tend to feel heavy after you've gone a few miles.

Actually, running shoes can be used for things other than jogging. They're good for any activity that involves the forward motion of the foot, such as walking, bike riding and ordinary day-to-day living.

When you're preparing to buy a pair, don't be misled by the terminology. Casual joggers should ask for either jogging shoes or training shoes. Marathon runners should ask for competition shoes or flats.

Now, then, ready to race around the block?

## Dirt vs. concrete

If you're a dirt jogger, you need less shoe cushioning. The earth is fairly easy on the feet. A waffle sole will give you good traction and is designed so that the dirt will not cling to the shoe.

If you're a concrete (pavement) jogger, you'll need more cushioning, as the sidewalk is hard on the feet. Waffles, nubs and studded soles are a waste of money for you. They'll wear down within a few weeks. An ordinary flat sole is best, any of the typical herringbone patterns will do. Granted, they won't give you as "soft" a run, but the shoes compensate for this with their durability.

# The perfect tennis shoe

When Gussie Moran appeared center court in lace-trimmed panties, she scandalized the tennis crowd. That was not the way to dress for this ultra-conservative sport. Nowadays, nobody would even bat an eye. Billie Jean King plays in rhinestones and sequins, Chris Evert serves in sexy halter tops and most of the men own shirts whose bold stripes match the color of their eyes. Television is partly responsible. Plain white glares, so most of the pros have switched to something more photogenic. That is, from the thighs up.

Their feet, however, are still in white. One would think there was an unspoken rule: Tennis shoes must be white or they won't be allowed on the court. Yes, a little colored trim is permissible, but the bulk of the

*Bobby Riggs entered the Robert F. Kennedy Pro-Celebrity Tennis Tournament disguised as Billie Jean King.*

shoe — white. The first person to challenge this will cause as much of a furor as Gussie did.

Tennis shoes are now available with three kinds of uppers: leather, canvas, nylon mesh. Leather shoes are, by and large, the most expensive, which is why many novices wait a while before trading up to them. On the positive side, they definitely give your feet the best support, which is something to think about seriously if balance is not your strong point. (Are you constantly knocking your ankle bones against each other? Do you trip over your feet frequently? Are you a "heavy" walker—that is, do you wear out a pair twice as quickly as most of your friends? Then leather may be the best choice for you.) On the negative side, leather is weightier. You have to expend more energy just to lift your feet up. By the end of the second set, you may be exhausted. Leather has also been criticized for its rigidity. You know what that means. The shoe has to be "broken in." It must be worn a few times before it conforms to your foot and flexes in the right places. As any anti-leather crusader will tell you, the material also has poor "breathing" ability. Your foot may get hot in the shoe, sweat and start to itch. Heavy perspirers might be better off with a more giving fabric.

Canvas uppers are lightweight and have excellent "breathing" aspects. Your foot will be comfortable in them. However, they will give it almost no support and, being so malleable, will lose their shape quickly.

Nylon mesh is a recent innovation, and right now manufacturers are putting most of their hopes behind it. After all, it's the new kid on the block. Realistically, you can expect some of the drawbacks of leather and some of those associated with canvas. But at the moment it's the best thing available for tennis players. An article in *The New York Times* recommended it over leather and canvas, and named Adidas, Bata, Cross-Court, Fred Perry and Tretorn as the most popular brands. At the Athlete's Foot, however, you won't hear such praise. Nylon mesh, they say, is put on a lot of *not* well-made shoes, which collapse at the slightest provocation. You have to be careful.

## Pivot action

To facilitate quick turning, look for a tennis shoe which is slightly beveled at the bottom of the toe and heel.

# Tennis aces

Courtesy New York Apples

Arthur Ashe,
Wimbledon winner.

*Billie Jean King, the powerhouse
behind the New York Apples,
World Team Tennis Champions.*

Courtesy New York Apples

*Vitas Gerulaitis,
a New York Apple.*

*Chris Evert, just
about unbeatable on clay.*

*Jimmy Connors, who wears tennies he designed himself.*

*Tracy Austin, named Rookie of the Year, 1977, by Tennis Magazine.*

**"** I wear a size thirteen. They call 'em 'the boats' on the circuit. **"**

**Stan Smith,** tennis star

Concerning tennis shoe soles, the most common bottoms are made of gum rubber, radial (a long-wearing, very dense rubber), polyurethane and an air-injected rubber (non-dense). First decide on your surface, then select the appropriate sole composition. For example, injected moldings are splendid on clay, but horrible on concrete. They wear out in nothing flat. Also, if you have a knee problem or any kind of leg ailment (from poor circulation to varicose veins to chronic weariness), radials and polyurethanes won't give you enough cushioning. Your leg will take too much pounding, so stay away from them.

The sole of a good tennis shoe is similar in structure to that of a good basketball shoe. It's wrapped around the shoe and designed for the lateral support needed by the leg and foot in a sport that concentrates on pivoting motions. (This is exactly contrary to the design of a good running shoe.) The point to be made here is not to wear a shoe engineered for forward motion (such as walking), but to buy one that's built on a side-to-side principle (the pivot).

The most frequently asked question regarding tennis shoes is What kind of padding do I need? Take as much as you can get. Look for a padded insole, padded tongue, padded collar. Look for a sturdy toe box with padding between it and the lining of your shoe (to prevent your toes from bashing against the edge). The more padding you have, the less likely you are to develop blisters. Give your feet that extra bit of comfort, if at all possible.

And don't forget to tell us if you start wearing maroon sneaks on the court. We want to be there when history's being made.

# Clay vs. hard-court

For clay (or grass) surfaces, you have to be able to slide through your shots. So you *don't* want a tennis shoe that has a deeply grooved sole. Shoes with injected moldings are usually good for playing on clay. The Tretorn, Adidas Nastase, Loveset and Fred Perry designs are all similar to each other and comfortable on clay or grass.

For hard-court games, you need a denser sole — perhaps a radial. Otherwise, you won't get enough traction and your shoe will wear smooth in nothing flat.

# sneaker fashion

# Kindergarten feet

Do you remember the first time you tied your shoelaces all by yourself? Chances are, those laces belonged to a pair of sneakers. And when you took them off and turned them over, there were your heroes — Batman, Superman, even Snoopy.

In New York, a cabby hung his kid's size twos from his rear-view mirror. He explained to his fares that they were his baby's booties. Sure enough, they even said it: "My first sneakers" was crayoned right on the uppers.

Shoes for the kindergarten set often resemble the back of cereal boxes. They act as ads for TV programs and often seem to be the handiwork of the Walt Disney studios. Snow White, it would seem, is fairy godmother to the sneaker industry, junior version.

Two of the more popular and durable brands of kids' sneaks come from Sears and Montgomery Ward, but Keds and Converse also feature a children's line. Boys and girls are not treated equally, however. Boy's sneaks are more practical, usually sporting toe bumpers and molded soles. Obviously, the Women's Lib movement hasn't filtered down this far, and girls are still expected to be less active than boys.

Spivak/Winn

## Why kids wear sneakers

Economy. Until a child is ten, it's quite likely he'll outgrow his shoes before he wears them out—and even then, according to the Podiatry Society of New York, he'll need a larger pair every three months. At the ripe old age of twelve, he might get away with four months to a pair, but that's not much less damaging to the pocketbook. Sneaks, inexpensive but sturdy sneaks, are the only answer to fast-growing feet.

# Storybook feet

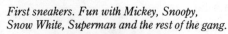

*First sneakers. Fun with Mickey, Snoopy, Snow White, Superman and the rest of the gang.*

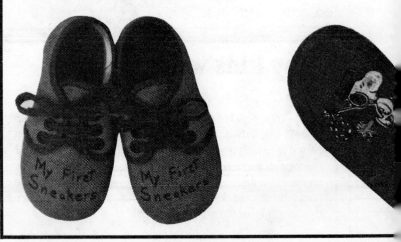

*The sneaker slip-on. Particularly nice if you haven't learned to tie yet.*

Peter Meltzer

115

# Schoolyard sneaks

**P**oor Amanda. There's this really cute boy she's dying to meet and he won't give her a second glance. He thinks she's involved. At *her* school, if you tie the laces so the bow is down near your toes, it means you're looking. At *his* school, it means just the opposite.

Matt's having his troubles, too. His Sperry Top-Siders were the rage of Newport, but now that he's moved to New York, all he hears is "Man, you gotta get some Cadillacs, Cadillacs for the feet."

Joyce still trembles when she remembers last year. Her team made the basketball playoffs, but when she saw her competitors' shoes, she knew her team had already lost. "They wore high-tops, you know," she said. "They were *tough.*"

If you want to learn about sneaker prejudice, hang around the schoolyard for a while. It's not enough to be wearing sneaks; you have to be wearing the *right* ones or you might as well go back to penny loafers.

For years, the inner-city street sneaks were Cons — it didn't matter whether they were black or white, or high or low-cut, just so long as they were made by Converse. But they're starting to take a back seat now that Pro-Keds has signed up Willis Reed of the Knicks to promote their line. (It also helps, of course, that their sole compound is specifically geared to pavement wear.)

*To make sure the knot doesn't unknot, double knot.*

# Graffiti

**A**n old (circa 1950) kind of popularity contest is making the rounds of the schools again. Who can get the most signatures on their sneaks. (The more names, the higher the status.) But there are little subtleties involved here. If *you* have to ask to write on kids' shoes, that's not so good. If *they* ask you, that's definitely big-time. *Where* you sign is important, too. The tongue area is reserved for a special friend. If that person pens a message as well as a name, you go to the head of the class. If, however, that person two-times you — signs the same thing, in the same place, on somebody else's sneak—you lose face.

The sneaker industry is not oblivious to this trend. In fact, they've capitalized on it with something called an "autograph sneaker," a stuffed toy sort of thing which is sold with a pen, and which winds up on your bed as a throw pillow.

Out in the suburbs, however, it's the reverse. Converse is out-ranking Pro-Keds.

Both companies sponsor traveling basketball clinics, but Pro-Keds has theirs in high school and college auditoriums whereas Converse holds theirs in hotels.

Hands down (an expression that turns out to be more appropriate than you might have suspected), the biggest sneaker craze now involves skateboard shoes, developed by Pepsi. The kids run through a pair every few weeks because the soles give out.

Still, some of the old school fads remain. Girls in the Midwest continue to try out for the cheerleading squad with pompoms tied to their sneaker laces and boys everywhere extol the virtues of basketball sneaks for everyday wear.

Amanda, on the other hand, has restrung her laces. Now if she'd just do something about her socks.

> **❝** I haven't worn sneakers since I was in high school because I associated them with gym. But I remember envying a teenage cousin who had Elvis Presley sneakers. I talked my grandmother into buying me some, but when we went to the shoe store they didn't have my size. I was distraught. **❞**
>
> **Fran Lebowitz,** author of *Metropolitan Life*

# The sneaker tote

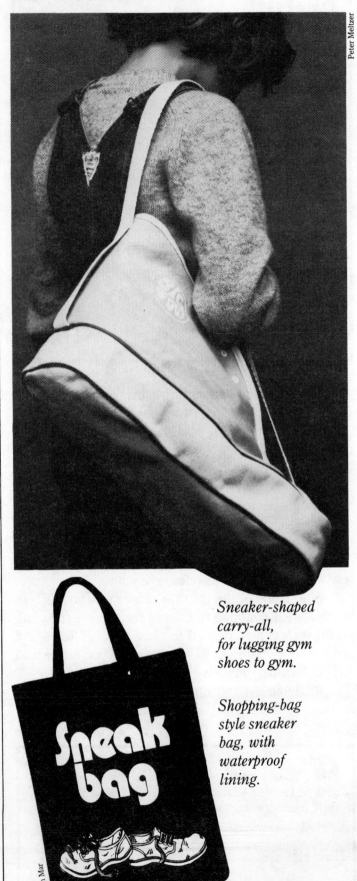

Peter Meltzer

© Fran Mar

*Sneaker-shaped carry-all, for lugging gym shoes to gym.*

*Shopping-bag style sneaker bag, with waterproof lining.*

# Sneaker swimwear

Courtesy Dorsay

*The Dorsay swim sneak.
(So your foot never touches the ooze.)*

*Miss Gloria
Swanson takes
the plunge
in calf-high
sneakers.*

United Press International

# Haute sneaker

**S**ome Cinderella story. It took sneakers over 100 years to get to the ball. Now you can't get them back to do the dirty work—like take out the garbage and clean the attic. After all, would you be quite so willing to get smudges on yourself if you had a famous designer's initials around your middle?

Betsey Johnson, the brightest design talent of the 1960's, was the first fashion specialist to see that the sneaker had possibilities. She thought it would be perfect with mini-skirts and floppy pants—if only it were a little taller. So she gave it a chunky heel, about two inches high and almost as wide. Soon after, not only were sneakers going to Beatles concerts but they were turning up as fashion plates in the pages of *Women's Wear Daily*. Mothers pawed through their daughters' closets in search of the newest "in" accessory. Once they found it, they wouldn't give it back.

Calvin Klein was the first "establishment" designer to work with sneakers. *Vogue* magazine was so enthusiastic about the results, it photographed him balancing a sneaker on top of his head, then splashed it across two color pages. Suddenly, sneakers became chic, and women who had snubbed them before now insisted on owning a pair. With the Klein label, naturally.

Marty Norman

# Custom sneakers

**I**f you fancy a pair of sneaks to match your mood, or a favorite outfit, you can pick your pattern and do-it-yourself with needlepoint. Two Needles, a New York shop specializing in the unusual, will send you a sneaker kit ($19 plus $1.50 postage) containing colorful wool yarn, uppers with prepainted patterns, and everything else that's needed to stitch up a design of flowers, strawberries, mushrooms, patchwork, paisley or rainbows. Return your artwork to the shop (1283 Madison Avenue, New York City), and they'll block the fabric ($1.50), have it made into a custom sneaker ($14) and mail back the finished product ($2.50 postage).

Van Doren Rubber Company performs the same service, but they'll also make sneakers out of other fabrics (everything except slippery fabrics like satin or waterproofed cloth, which don't take well to gluing). Van's makes clown shoes, too — those outrageously oversize sneakers—from the clown's own fabric, ranging from $25 to $50 (or more for a custom design). Best of all, if your feet are two different sizes, they'll supply you with a mixed-size pair at no additional charge. Query Van Doren Rubber Company, 704 East Broadway, Anaheim, Calif. 92805.

This year, just in time for what the fashion trade refers to as "the resort season," Geoffrey Beene introduced his version of a tennis shoe. Talk about class. It has a pale blue terry cloth lining, deep blue initials on the side ("GB") and a $30 price tag. As if that weren't enough, it came ambling along in its own lipstick-red fleece-lined tote bag. Beene swears the shoe was made to see clay court action, but when it's that beautiful and that expensive and designed by the hit of the Milan showings, who cares if it's functional?

Even Valentino whipped up a sneaker creation. One day Bianca Jagger (whose husband Mick wore sneaks to their wedding) looked in her closet, decided she had nothing to wear and rang up the famous couturier. She explained what she wanted, and he obliged: custom sneakers from a master craftsman. Can Halston and Dior be far behind?

Meanwhile, there are ready-to-wear sneaker wedgies, with satin uppers ranging in color from mauve to aubergine. When the disco strobes hit them, they look terrific. Shall we dance?

# Sneak chic

*The Sneaker T.*
For informal
moments.

*The Sneaker Maxi.*
Designed in Rome
for Henri Bendel,
New York
specialty
store.

Peter Meltzer

*The Status Sneakers.*
Shiny colored satin, with terrycloth lining.

*The Sneaker Pendant.* Strung from a lanyard.
(Often worn with the Sneaker T.)

*The Initial Sneak.*
Designed for tennis by
master couturier,
Geoffrey Beene.

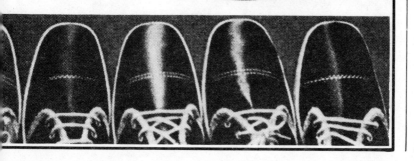

# The complete guide to men's sneaker fashion

Woody Allen escorted First Lady Betty Ford to a benefit performance marking the fiftieth anniversary of Martha Graham's dance troupe. He wore black sneaks, with white ties.

Rod McKuen announced the nominees for the Anthony Asquith Memorial Award, presented by the British Academy of Film and Television Arts, at the Royal Albert Hall, London. He, too, wore black sneaks, with white ties.

# Sneaker color war

**G**reen sneakers are a Celtics requirement. If you want to play, you wear them or suffer the consequences (a stiff fine). Take a good look at the team's feet the next time they're on the court. You'll see five shades of green out there. Seems each player orders his basketball shoes from a different manufacturer, and no two of them produce the same color. Another team in the NBA demands a certain color trim. The supplier doesn't make it, but he thoughtfully sends along Magic Markers so the team members can color in the stripe themselves.

Girls at a Chicago high school were so annoyed at a gym teacher's ultimatum— *You'll wear white sneaks in this class or find yourself in the principal's office!* — they all went out and bought navy blue ones, which they polished white just before class. Naturally, a lot of coats were needed to cover them. And since they were still wet, the sneaks left white streaks clear across the courtyard.

During the 1960's kids fought over Day-Glow. They'd take their white sneaks, spray paint them in the most garish combinations possible, then dress completely in black and go to a party. When they got up to dance (under black lights), it looked as thought there were acres of disembodied feet in the room.

## The razzle dazzle

To sew sequins on your sneaker, use an upholstery needle.

Peter Meltzer

# The sock controversy

## PRO: They look terrific.

## CON: They don't match.

# Lacing instructions

## Traditional

There are two ways to start. You can install the lace in the bottom pair of eyelets with the ends going *down into* the holes or coming *up through* the holes. Continue on either way, but don't switch methods mid-shoe. It looks just awful. The down-through-each-hole method makes somewhat showier, more distinct X's on top of the shoe, but the lacer is faced with the problem of having to change to the up-through-the-hole method at the last eyelet to make an effective tie at the end. Since this means sacrificing the final X, it's best to use this method on

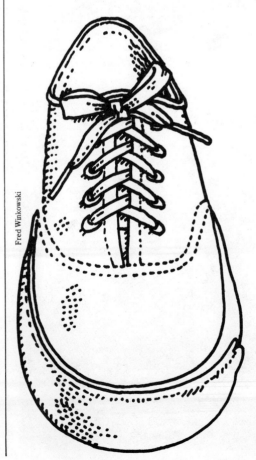

Fred Winkowski

shoes with plenty of eyelets. (On a four-hole-per-side sneaker, for instance, the total impression is confused and disjointed, with only two X's in a like direction.)

Note: Don't take just one lace at a time up to the top of the shoe, or you may finish with one side much longer than the other. Lacing connoisseurs consider this their greatest frustration. (Knots and tangles, after all, are an agreeable challenge.)

Most important of all: Always cross your X's the same way, either right over left, or left over right. It *is* acceptable—perhaps preferable—to do right over left on one sneaker and left over right on the other, in the pursuit of symmetry.

Think carefully before stringing bells on the laces.

Don't be afraid to use colorful laces. Most sneaks come into the world with white laces, but you needn't wait for these to wear out before changing them. Colors can be a way of asserting individuality, and regular changes are a tonic to the downtrodden spirit.

Make emergency lace-tips by tightly wrapping Scotch tape around the end of the lace. Poking a tipless end through an eyelet with a sharp object may only fray it further.

If you clean your sneaks in the machine, take the laces out first and hand-wash them (so they don't shrink).

# Horizontal

Insert the lace ends—both of them—into the bottom left and right holes, going *down into* the holes from above. Center the lace and pull ends taut — toward you.

Pause. Have some Gatorade.

Pass the left-hand lace tip *up* through the next left-hand hole. Pull taut.

Now take the right-hand lace end and pass it *up* through the *third* right-hand hole (always counting from the bottom).

Bring the left-hand end across to the second right-hand hole, and pass it *down* into the hole. Pull taut. (This is much, much easier if you do it as you read. Don't try to memorize instructions.)

Bring this *same end* —and don't lose track of it, now—*up* through the fourth right-hand hole. Pull taut.

Have another Gatorade. *Watch those loose ends.* You don't want to trip on the way back from the kitchen.

Take the end coming out through the third right-hand hole across to the third left-hand hole and pass it *down* into the hole. Pull taut. Pass it back *up* through the *fifth* left-hand hole.

Take the right-hand end across to the fourth left-hand hole and pass it *down* into that hole. Pull taut. Pass the same end back *up* through the sixth left-hand hole.

Now take the end coming through the *fifth* left-hand hole and bring it across and *down* into the fifth right-hand hole. Pull taut. Bring the same end *up* through the sixth right-hand hole.

Pull taut to adjust.

Tie laces. Replenish your Gatorade.

Note: This is also the preferred method for lacing L.L. Bean's Blucher Moccasin.

If you have more or fewer eyelets in your sneakers, adapt these instructions and go easy on the drinks. If you have an *odd* number, you can either skip the number one hole on each side or stop short of the top two.

Bear in mind that the ends called "right-hand" and "left-hand" exchange names frequently in these instructions, and do not necessarily keep the names they had when we started out.

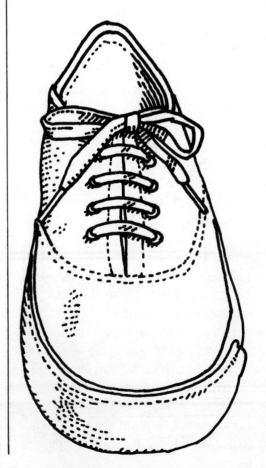

# Vertical

Put one end of the lace *down* into the first right-hand hole and bring it back *up* through the first left-hand hole. Pull taut and see that the ends are even.

Pass the left-hand lace-end *down* into the second left-hand eyelet, and *up* through the third left-hand hole. Repeat with the right-hand lace-end, using the corresponding right-hand holes.

Pass the left-hand lace-end *down* into the second left-hand hole, alongside the section of lace already running through the hole, and pull it tight. Watch out for trapped fingers. Bring the end back *up* through the third left-hand hole, then *down* through the fourth left-hand hole. Repeat these steps on the right-hand side.

Proceed — on each side — back *up* through the fifth, *down* through the fourth.

Now the challenging part. If your sneaker has six holes to a side, pass the lace *up* through the sixth hole, *down* through the fifth, and *up* through the sixth again, always remembering to pull taut. If you have five holes

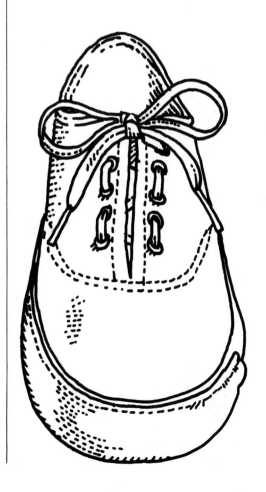

to a side, simply come back *up* through the fifth hole. If you have seven holes, come *up* through the fifth, *down* through the sixth, *up* through the seventh, *down* through the sixth again, and *up* through the seventh again. The point of all this is: The lace must finally be coming *up* through the final holes. (If you have fewer than five holes to a side or more than seven, you're on your own.)

Note: "Left" and "right" pertain to the wearer's left and right when the sneaker is on the foot.

This method is relatively useless for support of the foot, but it has a novel look. It also has the slim advantage of making the sneak easy to put on and take off quickly.

# Haphazard

No specific instructions — the essence of haphazard lacing is inspired improvisation.

Knots, however, are important to the effect. They should be tied as their section of the lace is being installed in the sneaker, *not* while the lace is separate (or the lace will be "locked out" of the holes). Remember: Knots never land where expected.

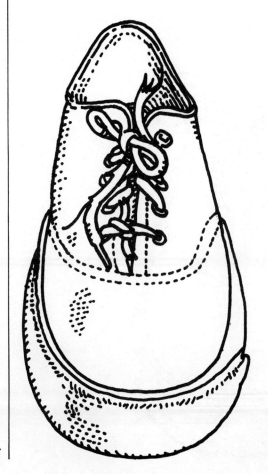

# Double-cross

Start the usual way, lace ends coming *up* through the first right and left eyelets. Pull taut and even. Cross each end to the second eyelet on the opposite side, and insert *down* into hole. Now cross each end to the other, original side, and come *up* through the third eyelet. Repeat instructions all the way up. If you have an even number of holes on each side, you may have trouble tying the lace since it is not coming *up* through the last holes. Therefore, you may need to skip the first or last holes in order to succeed. This looks best in ten-hole (five per side) sneakers.

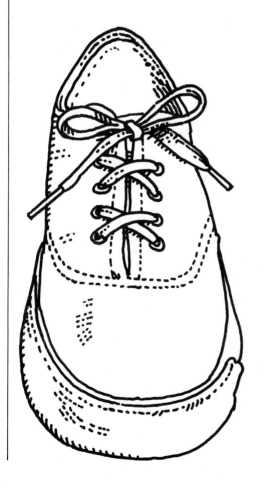

# Empty

Appropriate only if the sneaker is not to be worn.

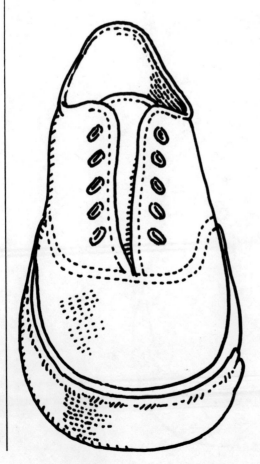

# Sneaker aesthetics

| Product | Rating | Comments |
|---|---|---|
| **Converse All-Stars:** | (4 sneakers) | The ultimate in sneaker classicism. Looks essentially the same today as it did in 1928. |
| **Keds Super Slip-Ons and Champion Oxfords:** | (1 sneaker) | Two low-cost classics. Virtually unchanged in this century. |
| **Adidas Country:** | (3 sneakers) | The "in" running shoe. Fast becoming the work shoe of the leisure class. |
| **Tiger Rotation:** | (3 sneakers) | Classically simple, but with complicated-looking features that scream athletic prowess. |
| **Pony California II:** | (1 sneaker) | Space Age design. Two-tone brown upper, with fluorescent orange everywhere else—laces, sole, lining. |
| **Imperial Century Pepsi Bowl Skate Shoe:** | (3 sneakers) | Matches the American flag. Unusual red foxing and toe cap. |
| **Nike Waffle Racer:** | (3 sneakers) | The most colorful sneaker, often with three or four strong hues on one shoe. |
| **Pro-Keds Night Hawk:** | (1 sneaker) | One of the sleeker designs around. A hot disco look. |
| **Adidas Official:** | (3 sneakers) | Made of fine leather for sports officials. A candidate for acceptability in the world of suits and ties. |

# The traveling sneaker wardrobe

**D**o you know how Europeans recognize American tourists? By their sneakers. If Americans aren't wearing them, they're talking about going back to the hotel to put them on. Since most guide books suggest comfortable shoes, and since this means only one thing to over 220 million United States citizens, sneaks are disgorged by the sightseeing busload — as ubiquitous as post cards, as mandatory as passports.

Experienced travelers have no trouble positioning them in their luggage: they compress the uppers (often by tying the shoes together with an extra pair of laces) and nestle the pair toe to toe. They cram the heels with travel necessities (Tums or wash-and-dry towelettes). En route, the sneaks rest in a hi-bulk sock, or a plastic bag, so as not to sully the souvenirs.

The knapsack set, on the other hand, wear one pair and sling any spares around their neck, love-bead style.

*En route to the Sneaker Museum.*

The classic traveling sneaker is spanking white, almost virginal. If it gets dirty during the day, the night finds it residing in a basin of Woolite. Tourists who do a lot of walking take along a runner's training shoe because of its extra-tough sole. Something like Etonic's Street Fighter, for example. Those who plan on softcore mountain climbing, tennis, squash or maybe a little basketball favor a solid multi-purpose design. To wit, Adidas' traditional training shoe.

With the advent of "theme" vacations—two weeks at a tennis clinic, a fortnight on a Windjammer cruise— holidayers have reevaluated their one-pair-is-plenty philosophy. They need multiples, in case the first pair wears out from overuse. And since they also must allow for the tour packager's complimentary cocktail hour, it's not uncommon to find them making room in the valise for sneakers with fancy brushed-suede uppers or satin high heels.

A little off the beaten track, but a must for wandering sneaker lovers, is the Bavarian mill town Herzogenaurach. Here, on the Adidas premises, is the only known sneaker museum. Admission is free. Down the road a piece is the Puma factory, also worth a visit.

*The Adidas Sneaker Museum, Herzogenaurach, Germany.*

# ¿Como se dice "sneaker"?

---

Arabic

---

Chinese

球鞋

---

French

tennis

---

Greek

Ἀθλητικά παπούτσια

---

Hebrew

נעל התעמלות

---

Japanese

運動ぐつ

---

Portuguese

tênis

---

Russian

ТЕНИСНАЯ ТУФЛЯ

---

142

# sneaker art

# The first sneaker gallery showing

**I**f you'd been walking west on New York's posh 57th Street in the spring of '74 and happened to glance in the window of No. 20, you'd have been smitten. There, larger than life, hung a framed portrait of a pair of sneakers. A discreet sign indicated that the Kornblee Gallery was presenting an exhibition called, simply enough, *Sneakers*. It ran for several months and was visited by thousands. Alas, gallery owner Jill Kornblee can't remember many details about the show, but she thought it was amusing, knows it was successful and is pleased she thought to mount it.

Selections from every art discipline were on view: oil, watercolor, acrylic, pen-and-ink, gouache, lithography, collage, soft sculpture.

There were frayed sneakers, holes-in-the-toes sneakers, sneakers piled on other sneakers, sneakers with two left feet, solitary sneakers, sneakers so realis-

Ferdinand Boesch

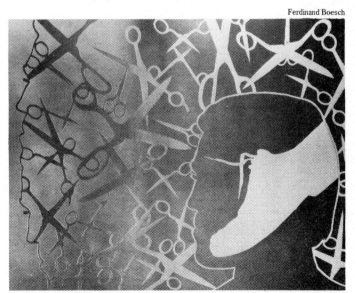

*From the Kornblee Gallery* Sneakers *Show, Lucas Samaras'* Cut Paper Drawing #52

tic they looked as if they could get up and walk away, sneakers that could only have existed in an artist's imagination.

If you're lucky enough to own a catalog from this show, hold on to it; it's a collector's item.

# The second sneaker show

S neakers again crashed the art world in April, 1978, as part of a foot retrospective held at the Museum of Contemporary Crafts in New York City. It included several fanciful sneakers, such as the tack-studded creation of Judith Auda and the Sun-Moon design of Louise M. Halsey.

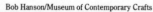
Bob Hanson/Museum of Contemporary Crafts

Sun-Moon Sneakers 1976: *Embroidery floss, satin-stitched wrapped, appliquéd, Louise M. Halsey*

Bob Hanson/Museum of Contemporary Crafts

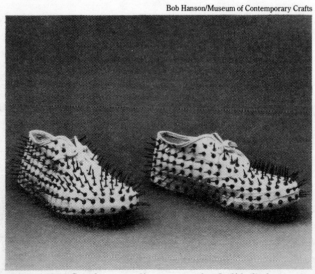

Untitled 1975 *Sneakers, acrylic, carpet tacks, Judith Auda*

# Harvey Kurtzman on sneakers

**"I**'ve drawn many sneakers. In fact, a recent Annie Fanny had a jogging adventure and I drew a record number. In one scene I have a million joggers. That's a lot of sneakers. I think I upped my sneaker output 50 percent on that one story."

*Mr. Kurtzman at his drawing board discussing Annie Fanny and the sneaker marathon.*

147

# Don Nice on sneakers

**"I** did my first sneaker painting in 1970. Out of that came a sneaker litho, my first experience with that form, in 1971. The painting that was in the Kornblee Gallery show was done in '73. Essentially, all of them were the same shoe — one I actually owned. It wasn't a particularly rational, planned choice. I do think,however, that it was the red stripe and blue stripe that got me interested. I just kept staring at them. They seemed to be as American as you can get."

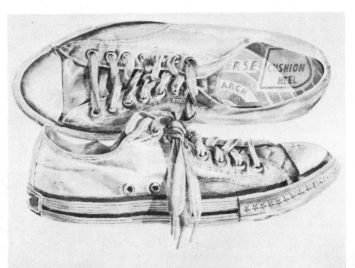

Double Sneaker, *acrylic on canvas.*

# Andy Warhol on sneakers

**"I** wear them to paint in. To make movies in. Actually, I wear them every day. I like them because they feel like you're wearing pillows.

I think I must have drawn sneakers when I was doing shoe ads, but that's so long ago I can't remember."

*Mr. Warhol, musing in a pair of Tiger sneakers.*

# John Holmstrom on sneakers

"**S**neakers are fun to draw. I put them on all my characters. But I remember when I was trying to get into the Cooper Union Art School, part of the test was to draw your feet in nine different poses. I was wearing sneakers, and needless to say, I failed the exam.

I'm addicted to sneakers — wearing them *and* drawing them. It's like having a real personality on your feet. When I was a kid, I thought they looked like they had little faces."

*Four-panel cartoon strip, pen and ink.*

# Sneaker sculpture

*Sneaker soft sculpture.*
*Canvas with bean bag cushion.*
*Sizes 4 to 6 feet.*
*(Can also be used as an*
*actual bed.)*

151

# Lowell Nesbitt on sneakers

**"I** could be a sneaker fanatic because of the fabulous colors they come in. I always notice the color of sneakers people are wearing, and I could go out and buy fifty at a clip—just to get all those colors.

When I was doing autobiographical work, I painted all my own shoes. I just took everything that was a shoe out of my closet. First I painted them lined up in an orderly row with the light things together and the boots in the back. Then I did the sneakers by themselves. Finally, I took the whole pile and threw them at random into a heap on the floor and did them that way.

They were in so many of my paintings, I felt bad about throwing them out. I always feel funny about objects that are in my work. But I tend to collect so many things, sometimes I just have to say 'Enough!'"

Courtesy Andrew Crispo Gallery

Collection of Shoes, *oil on canvas.*

# B. Kliban on sneakers

BKliban

---

# Douglas Kelley on sneakers

**"I** have a green pair of Pro-Keds that I wear every day. They earned me the nickname 'Green Sneakers' at a leading juvenile fashion magazine.

The worst thing about sneakers is wintertime and stepping in the slush. It's particularly pitiful to see a pair of Adidas that were once purple turned to black by city grime. What they should invent is the rubber-winterized, all-conditions sneaker."

153

# A sneaker retrospective

*Sneaker Relief,*
Ray Johnson.

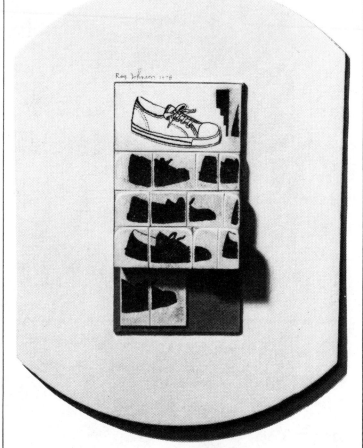

*David Winton, August 19,* Jennifer Mitchell.

*Keds*, Roy Lichtenstein, oil on canvas. (Wow.)

*Giant Gym Shoes,*
Claes Oldenburg.

*The Bicentennial Sneaker*, Stephen Varble

*The Grinner*, Peter Max.
(Mr. Max designed four
sneakers for the
Randy Manufacturing Co.
*The Grinner* sold over
one million pairs.)

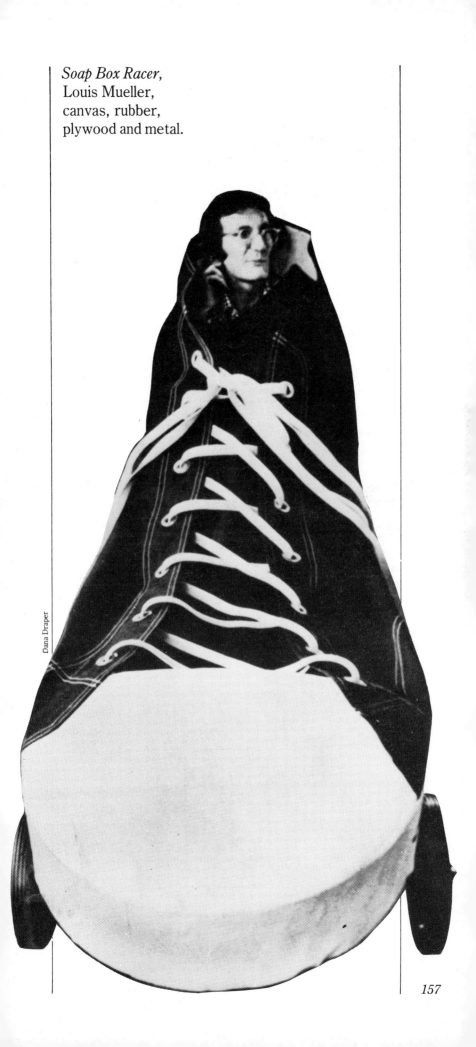

*Soap Box Racer,*
Louis Mueller,
canvas, rubber,
plywood and metal.

Dana Draper

# In praise of unknown artists

At the George Washington Middle School, West Hempstead, Long Island, students are still talking about their all-time favorite homework assignment. Art teacher Arlene Jacoby asked them to draw a picture of their sneakers. "Since you all seem to love them so much," she said, "and since you never take them off, use them as your model." The next day, 32 pencil sketches of sneakers appeared on her desk. These seventh and eighth graders weren't famous artists. Might not ever be. But could you do as well?"

*Artist*: Joseph Saracino

*Artist*: Phillip Goedel

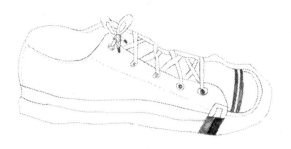

*Artist*: David Cayton

*Artist*: Santiago

*Artist*: Diane Cinquemani

*Artist*: Robert Brusco

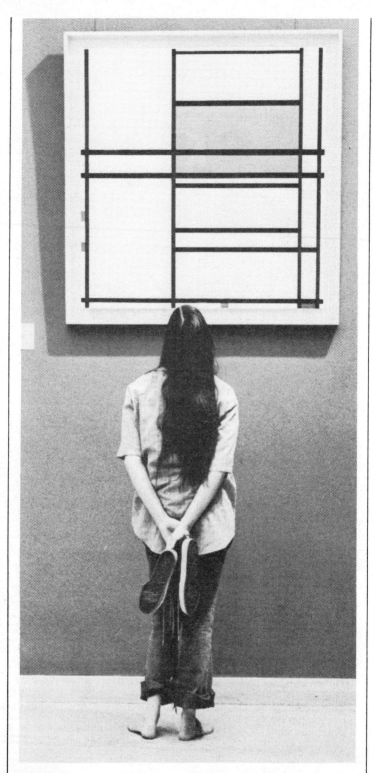

o you have any idea how many miles of corridor are contained in the Louvre? Or the Prado? Or the Museum of Modern Art? Unfortunately, if you try to cover them all in one day, you'll wind up foot-sore. Even if you're wearing sneakers. The best advice we can offer you is to do as Edward Gorey does. Walk right up to the painting you like, stare at it, then look around for the nearest bench and contemplate it from there.

# stage-struck sneakers

# Dancing feet

In the 1950's, television viewers were addicted to a program called *Omnibus*. It filled up most of their Sunday afternoon hours. One show was of special interest to sneaker fans. It starred Gene Kelly, who spent the better part of two hours discoursing on the similarities between the dance and athletics. For every step that took to the ballroom floor, he showed a complementary movement for the tennis court, the football field, the pitcher's mound, the skating pond. The world of sports seemed no less graceful than the world of dance, even though most of the athletes participated in sneakers.

So much for those who insist the sneaker is clumsy!

*Edward Villella rehearsing the* Dance of the Athlete.

Jacques d'Amboise, principal dancer with the renowned New York City Ballet, is currently preparing a similar television special, showing the relationship between the two disciplines. So sneaker fans can again expect to see rubber-soled twinkletoes on the small screen.

In a similar vein, the ballet *Dance of the Athlete* features a *pas de deux* with a ballerina *en pointe* and her partner more solidly (though nonetheless handsomely) anchored in sneakers. Edward Villella recently danced the role—with several horizontal bands of tape placed over his sneaks' laces to make sure the shoes didn't slip. (Even this has a ballet parallel. Ballerinas make sure their toe ribbons don't slide by cementing them to their tights with Elmer's Glue.)

Sneaks are no strangers to the Broadway stage either. Remember *West Side Story?* Here come the Jets, yeah, and here come the Sharks, and both gangs were in sneakers. And when the movie was made, there were the sneaks again, larger than life and in Technicolor.

Martha Swope

*Jerome Robbins shapes up the Jets and the Sharks.*

*Grease,* the long-running off-Broadway musical about growing up in the 1950's, had all the girls in the cast wearing sneakers and gray felt skirts with poodle appliqués, and we can expect to see the same footnotes in the movie version.

The award-winning *A Chorus Line* featured one Broadway hopeful in sneakers. As she explained to the show's "director," she wore them to auditions because her feet hurt from waiting so long for it to be her turn.

The newest dancing feet belong to *The Runaways.* Ads for the musical showcase a large sneaker autographed by cast members (who dance in them onstage).

Jazz is the one legitimate dance form that often uses sneakers onstage. This came about because the roots of jazz, like those of rock music, sprang up in the streets. Jazz dancers, like many other dancers, almost always wear sneaks in rehearsal. They use them to practice in because they have better traction on slippery floors. (An interesting note is that jazz dancers also sprinkle Ajax and Coca-Cola on their dance floors to make them more skidproof.)

Sneakers have even been known to win dance contests. Most of the finalists in the Harlem Harvest Moon Jitterbugging Contest had them on their feet, as well they might — since the activity required more traction than basketball.

Courtesy Twyla Tharp

*Twyla Tharp's* Mud. *The first, third and fifth movements are performed in sneakers.*

In the early 50's, many schools required sneakers at the Friday night Hop. This was because the gym floor had just been shellacked for the Big Game the next day.

# Sneaker goes to Hollywood

**M**ind you, we don't have real proof, but it's our understanding that sneakers have taken part in many of the major cinematic love scenes. The stars were photographed in fancy evening dress or period costumes, but only from the waist up. Since they were out of camera range, the wardrobe department ignored their feet. They were decked out by the actors themselves. In sneakers.

Of course, sneakers have actually made it to the silver screen in such productions as *They Shoot Horses, Don't They?*, a film about marathon dancers during the

*Jane Fonda and Michael Sarrazin in* They Shoot Horses, Don't They?

Depression. Almost the entire cast was outfitted in black high-tops, like the good old P. F. Flyers basketball shoes. Recently, sneaks have been experiencing the old typecasting problem. If the script calls for a Cloud Nine locale, up they go. George Burns got to wear them in *Oh, God,* and Warren Beatty will soon be seen in them in *Heaven Can Wait* as an angel who was formerly a track star. The film company has issued a poster of Mr. Beatty as he appears in the movie—with large white wings, a pale gray sweatsuit and a pair of running shoes. They can hardly keep up with the demand for them.

In their off-hours, the stars rely on their sneakers as much as on their agents. Lee Majors and Farrah Fawcett-Majors jog in them, Steve Allen and Jayne Meadows play tennis in them and Paul Newman sips Coors in them. And back in the days when Charlie Chaplin was playing the Little Tramp, he liked to wear them over to Pickfair, the palatial digs of his good friend Douglas Fairbanks, Sr. and Mary Pickford.

When Howard Hughes decided to dabble in films, he could afford to be a little eccentric. (Who couldn't, owning half the money in the world?) He bought the RKO studio, and visitors to the back lot often found him seated in the director's chair watching over his

*This may or may not be Howard Hughes, but these are certainly his sneakers.*

*This is certainly Farrah Fawcett-Majors.
You can tell by her sneakers.*

productions. He refused, however, to dress in typical director fashion — riding breeches and shiny leather boots. Instead, Hughes preferred knickers, Argyle kneesocks and sneakers. Later, stories would circulate that his idea of appropriate footgear was any one of three things; sneakers... shoe boxes... or nothing.

Regardless, if you're asked to sign a movie contract and succeed in becoming a big star, don't forget your "old friends." Precedent has been set. And you may rest assured that your sneaks will feel right at home in the Hollywood Hills. | 169

# The sneaker comedy routine

## by Professor Irwin Corey

"**M**y first involvement with the somewhat distinguished apparel was based on the assumption that the attitude must be maintained in order to clarify that which can be cleared up with ease rather than with talent. In order for us to appreciate, we must dissolve the cloak of rhetoric and go right into the main functions of whatever the apparatus can do. And we realize projectedly that we can only focus our attention into the areas which seem to be subjective, and that to look at anything objectionable would be somewhat of a defensive attitude. Therefore, we must relate on that plane to develop a new posture whereby we can accept whatever the new contributions might be, regardless of the area or locale or given identity to the proposition. When you get right down to the basic fundamental rudiments, there can only be a reservoir for an understanding, and the longer the understanding the firmer the grip. What is intimated here is that one is obligated to accept this formula. Outside of that fact, people can just go nude."

---

### Sneaker thief

"**I**'ve been wearing them since the time somebody stole my shoes at the Palmer House in Chicago. To go onstage without *some* sort of footgear would have been inappropriate, so I put my sneakers on.

When I was working at the Hungry i in San Francisco, part of a local college's fraternity initiation was to get Professor Corey's sneakers. They'd already been stolen by the time some kids showed up and asked for them, so I just said, "Buy a pair and I'll say they're mine." **Professor Corey**

# The singing sneak

**C**arnivorous Records 1 has just produced the first Sneakers' album. Named for the best-loved footwear in the world, the group includes Rob Slater and Chris Stamey on guitar, Robert Keely on bass, Will Rigby on drums, Mitch Easter on acoustic guitar, and Chris Chamis and Robert Kirkland on percussion. They write all their own songs, and if you had to label them, you'd be safe saying they were in the punk rock idiom.

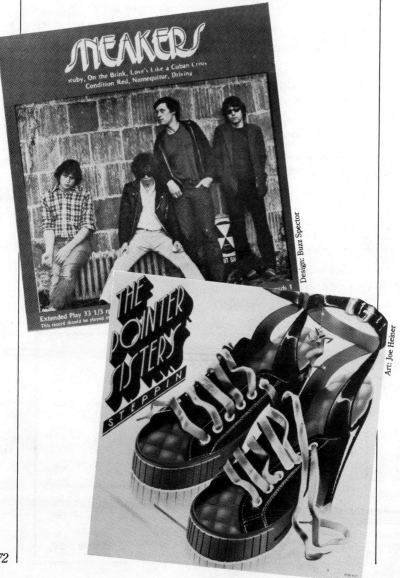

Design: Buzz Spector

Art: Joe Heiner

Punk rockers are partial to sneakers. In Britain, they do their stuff in Converse All-Stars, Pro-Keds high-tops and Dunlop plimsolls. American punks like Connies, too, but also plain white, low-cut Keds meant for tennis, boating slip-ons and exotic orange and green cheapies made in Korea.

Says Adny Shernoff, bassist and songwriter of The Dictators, "To be honest, sneakers have always been my favorite footwear. I have high black Converse and high white Converse, and then I have a dirty pair which I wear if I'm jogging or something. Then I have a fancy pair of sneakers for when I go out on a date. Since I've gotten out of high school, I've had sneaks on my feet 95 percent of the time. I was just in England and

## Who writes the songs?

"**W**ould you believe this is my first pair of sneakers? For real. Ah-dee-dahs ... I know: Adidas! You see, I wasn't very athletic as a kid. I never had a baseball, never had a football, never had a basketball... It was always 'Barry, practice!'"

**Barry Manilow**

Second Barry Manilow Special, ABC-TV, February 24, 1978

saw Joe Strummer of The Clash, and he'd just gotten a new pair of black Converse high-tops. He was really proud of them. They're really the only thing to wear on your feet as far as I'm concerned."

(Although Shernoff didn't mention it, perhaps one reason so many rockers like sneaks is that they provide good grounding when you're working with high-powered electrical instruments.)

*Adny's Adidas*

Barry Manilow chose to wear sneaks on his second TV special, and Bruce Springsteen, the cult figure who hit big a year or so ago, featured them on the cover of his *Born to Run*.

And you can guess what's on the feet of nearly every rock groupie as she chases her favorites to their limousine door.

Sneakers' popularity with the rocker set, and to a lesser degree with the pop music contingent, is no surprise. After all, rock music has a "street-wise" reputation. Its musicians are often from crowded urban centers, which for years have been prime sneaker territory. So naturally, when the rock groups got famous, they took their old friends along.

# High-Heel sneakers

*Put on your red dress ba-by,*
*'Cause we're go-in' out to-night;*
*Put on your red dress ba-by,*
*'Cause we're go-in' out to-night;*
*And wear some box-ing gloves in case some fool might wan-na*
*fight.*

*Put on your High-Heel Sneakers,*
*Wear your wig hat on your head;*
*Put on your High-Heel Sneakers,*
*Wear your wig hat on your head;*
*I'm pret-ty sure now ba-by you know you're gon-na knock 'em*
*dead.*

*Put on your High-Heel Sneakers,*
*Wear your wig hat on your head;*
*Put on your High-Heel Sneakers,*
*Wear your wig hat on your head;*
*I know you re-a-lize — pretty sure you're gon-na knock 'em*
*dead.*

*Tommy Tucker*

**W**ant to croon a love song to your sneaks? There happens to be one, sort of. Written by rhythm-and-blues man Tommy Tucker, it was the No. 1 hit of 1964, and his version of it sold more than a million copies. Says Tucker about the song's origin, "Initially, hi-heel sneakers was a joke. It was part of a kid's insult game called 'dirty dozens.' One kid would say, 'Your mother wears combat boots,' and the other kid might reply, 'Your mother wears hi-heel sneakers.'"

Although the song was intended as a spoof, it remains one of the most recorded songs of all time. Some of the artists who helped keep it on the charts were:

| | |
|---|---|
| Chuck Berry | Johnny Hallyday |
| Freddy Cannon | Roland Kirk |
| The Chambers Brothers | Jerry Lee Lewis |
| John Davidson | Chuck Mangione |
| Sammy Davis, Jr. | Elvis Presley |
| The Everly Brothers | Boots Randolph |
| Jose Feliciano | Johnny Rivers |
| Eddie Floyd | Ike and Tina Turner |
| Bill Haley and the Comets | Stevie Wonder |

# Sneak rock

The wedding of Mr. and Mrs. Mick Jagger.
He wore sneakers. She did not.

The Ramones,
your average,
clean-cut,
punk rock group.

The long-playing
sneaker.

Ron Pownall

© Roberta Bayley

Boston *amplification
system: more sparkles.*

Graham Parker on stage
*in running shoes.*

© Roberta Bayley

*Alice Cooper looks lovely in sneaks. He accessorizes them with hand-hemmed jeans and a hand-held beer bottle. His sneaker secret? White shoe polish.*

# Sneaker poetry

The makers of Converse ran a poetry contest for people between the ages of eight and eighteen. Over $1000 in prize money was awarded. We proudly present some of the winners.

## Jive to my sneakers

*I sometimes wonder how sneakers came to be.*
*Did Washington wear them?*
*Did General Lee?*
*Did Betsy Ross wear them, when she wasn't wearing slippers?*
*Did Davy Jones, when he couldn't find his flippers?*
*Did Christopher Columbus and Queen Isabella,*
*    wear their sneakers when they danced the Tarentella?*
*Did Paul Revere wear sneakers, as he made his famous ride?*
*Was Alexander Hamilton wearing sneakers when he died?*
*I wonder!!!!*

—Deirdre Sillivan and Bette Sullivan, Age ten, Douglaston, New York

## The soft and gentle sneaker

*I'd rather be a guy in jeans than in a suit and shirt*
*I'd rather be a girl in pants than nylons and a skirt*
*I'd rather farm than live where earth is scarce and plants are few*
*I'd rather wear a sneaker than a shoe.*

*I'd rather hike in mountains than in cities' festering noise*
*I'd rather give my kid some clay than guns and warfare toys*
*I'd rather work by planting trees than on an airforce crew*
*I'd rather wear a sneaker than a shoe.*

*I'd rather drink a glass of milk than kill a baby lamb*
*I'd rather eat an apple than a slaughtered piglet's ham*
*I'd rather not use leather, which a cow's live body knew*
*I'd rather wear a sneaker than a shoe.*

Jessica Wolin, Age seventeen, Roslyn, New York

# Owed to my sneakers

I owe my childhood sneakers almost nothing,
Even though they were supportive, loyal friends.
My laces used to knot,
And I'd step in gum a lot,
Setting all the most unpleasant sneaker trends.

My teenage sneakers marched me in the sixties.
They kept me on my toes, awake but numb.
I relied upon my Keds,
To help outrace the Feds,
And to mark the beat of "We Shall Overcome."

I owe my college grades, in part, to sneakers.
It's time the truth was out and praises sung.
Those days it was the norm,
As we studied in the dorm,
To scribble answers underneath the tongue.

As a grownup I crave many pairs of sneakers,
But they're sold at higher prices I abhor.
Pairs for jogging, tennis, dress,
Make my finances a mess,
So I clone them. I'm not buying any more.

**Suzanne Rafer**

# sneaker care

# The Saturday night bath

The next time you step in the shower, you might consider taking your sneaks in there with you. After all, they get dirty, too. If you think that's only for sissies, we refer you to George Brett, third baseman for the Kansas City Royals, who admits, without a trace of blush, that he routinely scrubs down his sneakers. "I just take out the laces and wear them in the shower," he says, "or throw them in the washing machine."

Cleaning via the shower method is easy, if you're nimble. You brace your shoe in one hand, clasp your nail brush in the other, then make contact — bringing the brush to the shoe, not vice versa.

Washcloths and loofas won't work. The first are too floppy and the second usually disintegrate mid-shoe, leaving you to sidestep bits of sponge which booby-trap the floor. (Stick with your nail brush.)

If your footwear seems particularly rank, you might switch to a bar of deodorant soap for the occasion.

Just before you exit the tub, sit on its edge and remove both sneaks. Now tackle their soles. Don't try to do this while balancing on one foot; you might wind up with your leg in a cast.

Wash the laces separately by pummeling them between your hands. When they're spotless, reinsert them, tie their ends together loosely, and use them to swing the sneaks over the shower curtain rod. Let the sneaks hang there for a full twenty-four hours so they won't be wet and clammy when you put them on.

Washing machine procedure is even easier, since it involves absolutely no manual labor (or dexterity) on your part.

Set the machine to the hot-water cycle.

Sprinkle in soap powder. This once, forget about using bleach or fabric softeners.

Load the washer, putting white sneaks with white clothing, colored ones with dark things — jeans, for example. Otherwise, you might discover you have navy blue jockey shorts.

Never wash sneaks by themselves. They'll bounce

United Press International

*The tub flub: Sneaks on the grass do not get as clean as sneaks in the water.*

around the machine, which is not so good for them or the washer.

Now go amuse yourself for a half-hour until your laundry's done. That's all there is to it. (Except, of course, the reminder that you can't put sneaks in an automatic drier. Clothespin them to the line instead.)

We do know of meticulous types who iron their shoelaces, but frankly we think that's overdoing it.

*The tub scrub.*

# Machine wear-and-tear

**W**e've all heard the argument that it's wiser to wear dirty sneaks than to let them take their chances in the washer. The people at Sears, however, regularly test sneakers for durability by sending them through the machine a minimum of ten times. If it gobbles them up, it's not the machine that's at fault; it's the sneak. Your sneaker *should* withstand the pressure of machine washing. If it doesn't, it's not of very good quality.

Some people refuse to clean their sneaks at all. Ever. If they happen to be under fifteen, this is excusable. They'll outgrow them before they get truly filthy. But we have little tolerance for the weekend athlete who exercises maybe two or three hours total, then tries to convince himself he's in good shape because his sneaks got dirty. He figures he's quite a sport and uses his smudged sneaks to back him up.

On the other hand, there's one group of people who wouldn't dream of washing sneaks or of wearing dirty ones: minor functionaries in the New York Mafia. According to a noted criminal lawyer who makes a career of defending these gentlemen (he declined to give his name, or theirs, for that matter), the middle-level Mafioso wears a pair of sneakers until the first black spot appears. Then he throws them out and buys new ones. It's not uncommon for a man of this type to buy a new pair every week.

Think of that the next time you're tempted to let yours stay dirty.

# Repairs: professional

**S**wish, swish, flop. Swish, swish, flop. Sound familiar? That's the Dangling Sole Three-Step. As the gap between the top and the bottom of your sneaker widens, you develop a peculiar gait. It's part glide, part shuffle, and its point is to keep your feet flat on the floor. If you raise them, your sneak will go in contrary directions: the upper takes off skyward (begging for help?) and the sole bends back to trip you.

When sneakers were merely sneaks (less than $10) and reached this state, they were strictly disposable. But now that they boast fancy names (and $40 price tags), a whole sneak repair industry has developed. The little shoemaker at the corner who refurbishes your wing-tips may now also revitalize your sneaks. If he doesn't, you can mail them in to sneak repair specialists who will treat them to new soles, new laces, new insoles and arch supports, mending, relasting and, for white shoes, paint jobs. Approximate cost: $15.

One caveat—vulcanized models (shoes with the soles and uppers bonded together) may not be reclaimable.

## Sneak repairers

**Nu-Buttoms.** (426 Hillside Ave., Williston Park, N.Y. 11596). Will repair and restore entire shoe for $12.95; simple resoling, $9.50.

**Resole.** (1169 Sonora Ave., Sunnyvale, Calif. 94086). Specializes in Adidas; offers Adidas factory soles—or, for other shoes, the best soles available. Resoling and reconditioning, $13.95 plus $1.50 postage (add 40¢ for new laces).

**Spare Pair.** (38–42R Everett St., Boston, Mass. 02134). Rebuilds New Balance, Adidas, Puma, Nike, Tiger, Brooks, Tretorn, K-Swiss, Fred Perry, Etonic, Lydiard, Uniroyal and Spot Bilt. Cost, $13.95.

Courtesy We Resole Sneakers Inc.

*Before.*　　　　　　　*After.*

**We Resole Sneakers.** (684 Third Ave., New York City, 10017). Will repair anything, but specializes in Adidas, Puma, Tiger, Tretorn, Nike, Head, Converse and Hyde.

# Repairs: amateur

**T**he more disreputable the sneaker, the more some people love it. They don't consider it "broken in" until both heels are suitably frayed, there's a small rupture on the left upper which lets the big toe emerge, the eyelets have dislocated their metal rings, the laces are knotted in at least two places and it's impossible to determine the shoe's original color.

To some, this spells chic.

And they'll do anything to hang on to a sneak in this condition, including doctoring it with safety pins (diaper pins, if it's a really big rip), Scotch tape, needle and thread (which they wield in a drunken Kamikaze flight pattern), paper clips, rubber cement, rubber bands, Elmer's glue, library paste, chewing gum (replaced daily), string, twine and left-over party streamers.

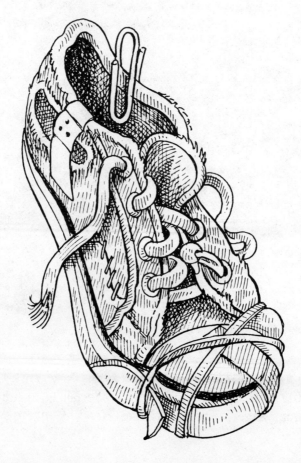

Marty Norman

# Shoe patch and shoe goo

These two products (yes, they're both proper names) can prolong the life of the threadbare sneaker. What they are, very simply, is wax, which you insert in an electric shoe gun. Just apply the heated wax to thin spots (think of putting on several coats of nail polish) and let harden overnight. But be careful not to dribble.

None of which keeps the shoe from eventually falling apart, but never mind; the fact that they tried is all that matters. (We suspect they're the same ones who, in childhood, had a hard time relinquishing their teddy bears, and as adults, never seem to know when the love affair's over.)

These incorrigible do-it-yourselfers obey an eleventh commandment: Thou shalt not throw out thy sneaker. It's up to a stronger, braver member of their household to take the thing out and bury it.

The only exception we know of is a decrepit-sneaker owner who thought he could patch up his old friend with a few strategically-placed staples. Only trouble was he forgot to take his foot out first. Right after he got his tetanus shot, he tossed away his sneakers all by himself. Maybe next time he'll think of using masking tape.

The town of Montpelier, Vermont, thinks sneaks in their last stages have a sort of perverse glory. And every year they honor them with a "Rotten Sneakers" contest. Recently, entries have been so flamboyantly tattered, it was a miracle they could make their way to the judging area. First prize? What else? A new pair for the winner to start working on.

# Gripping power

Scrunch up your toes. Now try to pick up a pencil with them and walk across the room with it. If you can master this exercise, you'll have developed sufficient "gripping power" to control your wayward sneaker soles without recourse to rubber bands, rubber cement or the local repair service. If you can't, buy a new pair because you certainly won't be ambulatory in the old ones.

# The odor problem

**T**ake a good whiff. Not exactly roses, is it?

Sneaks, sorry to say, often smell worse than a backyard privy. Small wonder. You play a hard game in them, then shut them up in an unventilated cubicle. The least you could do is put them on top of your locker to air out. (Don't worry about somebody stealing them. You could always track the culprit by following your nose.)

If you'll remember, the sneaks didn't start out quite so rank. That was your doing. You perspired into them. The thing to bear in mind here is that if you didn't, you'd be a candidate for intensive care. Perspiration is the body's cooling mechanism, without which we'd all be burning up.

Still, it would be nice if someone invented a foot deodorant that really worked. Unfortunately, no one has. Ergo, the Odor Problem.

The best solution seems to be frequent baths, for you *and* your sneakers.

A liberal dousing of after-shave or toilet water is ineffective. And expensive.

Sweat socks don't actually retard odors, but they do appear to absorb them, thereby saving your sneaks from contamination. Deodorant socks (Bonnie Doon and Interwoven are two of the several brands available) provide a short-term solution; unfortunately, their effectiveness seems to give out in the wash.

Most five-and-dime stores offer Odor Eater inner soles, which supposedly trap the scent in a charcoal filter. You may not find them totally successful, but they do give your feet a little extra cushioning.

One suburban mother in Summit, New Jersey, helped solve the odor problem by the rotation principle. She bought each of her kids three pairs of sneaks and wouldn't let them wear A again until they'd given B and C an outing. Said she: "That way, the sweat doesn't accumulate. It gets a chance to dry out. And I don't worry about bad smells any more."

Another possibility is to wear sneaks with mesh uppers. Hopefully, the smell will waft through the openwork.

# The deep-six

**U**ltimately, we've all got to say it: Goodbye, old friend. Sneaker disposal is a highly charged, emotional thing, often characterized by tears, sobs and eyes shut tight to obliterate the pain. Still, it must be done. Six common elimination methods are:

**1. The Aerial.** This high-wire act is a teenage favorite. At the end of the school year, the gang assembles at the street corner, motley sneakers in tow, and each member takes a turn at heaving his pair over the traffic light bracing. (The more you respect your sneakers, the closer to the actual lights you'll try to place them.) The sneaks then hang there until they decay. In some neighborhoods, this is called the rite of "wiring."

Bert Miller

**2. The Burial.** This ceremony occurs within the confines of the home and is thought to be Egyptian in origin, in that the deceased are entombed with symbols of their former life (the odd sock or two, an old tennis racket cover, a deflated basketball). The sneaks are either stashed under the bed or in the back recesses of the closet, where they're available if you need to thwack a stray bug. The method's prime advantage is that it lets you visit your sneaks periodically, to relive past glories.

**3. The Ersatz.** In which you only *pretend* to banish your sneakers. Let's say an older, tougher, less sentimental family member has suggested you get rid of them or forget about dinner. You stuff them under your shirt and cart them off to school, where they live out their old age in your gym locker.

**4. The Immortal.** In which you preserve them for posterity by a process known as bronzing. Only for the very rich (or foolishly extravagant), bronzing starts at $40. For further information, contact Endurart, 259 West 30th St., New York City.

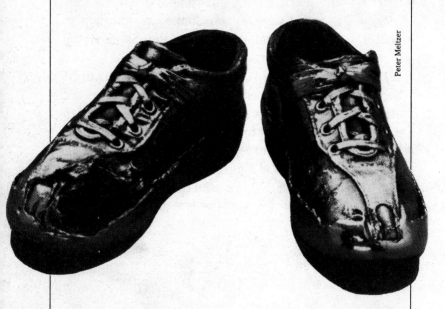

Peter Meltzer

**5. The Legacy.** The method involving the active participation of another. The sneaks are dropped in the nearest litter basket, swaddled in newspaper, in hopes that the local shopping bag lady will excavate them.

**6. The Eternal Triangle.** In which your old friends finally end up with your best friend: Fido (who's coveted them for years). This is a two-stage program. First, you and Fido play catch. You throw, he retrieves. Next, you throw, he catches but he hangs on to them with his incisors. Bye-bye, old friends.